UNIVERSITY OF NORTH CAROLINA AT CHAPEL HILL
DEPARTMENT OF ROMANCE LANGUAGES

NORTH CAROLINA STUDIES
IN THE ROMANCE LANGUAGES AND LITERATURES

Founder: URBAN TIGNER HOLMES

Editor: MARÍA A. SALGADO

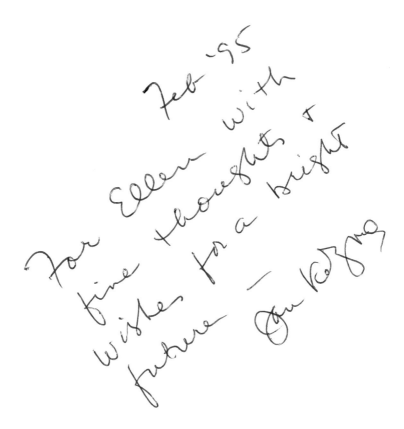

Distributed by:

UNIVERSITY OF NORTH CAROLINA PRESS

CHAPEL HILL

North Carolina 27515-2288

U.S.A.

NORTH CAROLINA STUDIES IN THE
ROMANCE LANGUAGES AND LITERATURES
Number 244

THE ARCHITECTURE OF IMAGERY
IN ALBERTO MORAVIA'S FICTION

THE ARCHITECTURE
OF IMAGERY IN
ALBERTO MORAVIA'S FICTION

B Y

JANICE M. KOZMA

CHAPEL HILL

NORTH CAROLINA STUDIES IN THE ROMANCE
LANGUAGES AND LITERATURES
U.N.C. DEPARTMENT OF ROMANCE LANGUAGES

1 9 9 3

Library of Congress Cataloging-in-Publication Data

Kozma, Janice M.
The architecture of imagery in Alberto Moravia's fiction / by Janice M. Kozma.
p. – cm. – (North Carolina studies in the romance languages and literatures; no. 244)
Includes bibliographical references and index.
ISBN 0-8078-9248-3
1. Moravia, Alberto, 1907- –Style. I. Title. II. Series.
PQ4829.062Z72   1993

853'.912–dc20   92-56385
                                                        CIP

ISBN 0-8078-9248-3

IMPRESO EN ESPAÑA

PRINTED IN SPAIN

DEPÓSITO LEGAL: V. 2.348 - 1993   I.S.B.N. 84-599-3309-1

ARTES GRÁFICAS SOLER, S. A. - LA OLIVERETA, 28 - 46018 VALENCIA - 1993

TABLE OF CONTENTS

ACKNOWLEDGEMENTS

I wish to acknowledge the generosity of The University of Kansas for awarding me a sabbatical leave and General Research Grants (numbers 344-XX-0038 and 3672-XO-0038) to complete this work. Note: a version of Chapter V appeared in *Italica* 61.3 (1984): 207-19. I want to thank especially my good friend and colleague, Roberta Johnson, for her meticulous editorial advice and for her invaluable insights and thoughtful suggestions. Finally, I dedicate this study to my mother, Maria Pedica-Kozma, and to the memory of my father, William Kozma, my two favorite supporters.

O body swayed to music, o brightening glance,
How can we know the dancer from the dance?

William Butler Yeats,
"Among School Children" (1927)

I

INTRODUCTION

OLINDA: Metafora? Mi spieghi questa parola.
MILONE: Metafora è una figura retorica che sulla base di una similitudine rimanda a un oggetto diverso da quello nominato.
OLINDA: Che bello, che bello, mi dia un esempio di metafora.
MILONE: Per esempio: la famiglia, questa pietra angolare dell'edificio della società. In questo caso, pietra, parola di solito sana, diventa malata, malatissima.
OLINDA: Questa è una metafora?
MILONE: Della più bell'acqua.
OLINDA: Che bello, che bello. Lei dovrebbe spiegare queste cose così belle alla prossima riunione.

Il mondo è quello che è
Alberto Moravia (55-56)

Literature tries to rearrange random experience in order to produce a useful code for living; an author organizes chaotic events, problems, encounters, thoughts, concepts, etc., into fixed, written form in an effort to make human sense of them. In doing this, the narrator functions much like the lens of a camera. S/he fixes upon a predetermined, limited view, and (to extend the convenient metaphor), in the "darkroom" with the writing instruments, s/he makes some very conscious choices: perhaps cropping the view, highlighting or darkening the tones, allowing a greater or lesser amount of light to shine upon the image to deepen or de-emphasize certain parts of the picture. The result (for both writer and photographer) is a thoroughly manipulated recreation of that first raw image conceived respectively through the lens of the camera and the fictive imagination.

In most cases the author's final "picture" wants to present itself as some form of "reality," but in fact it is as controlled and refashioned as s/he cares to make it. If successful, the outcome will help the reader draw meaning from and deal with the seemingly chaotic, random experiences of life. There are as many means as there are authors to present a literary rearrangement of "reality"; that means, that vehicle is shaped by the author's style, what Roland Barthes calls "the writer's thing, his glory" (*Writing Degree Zero* 11).

Ironically the general consensus in Italian criticism seems to be that Alberto Moravia's style is straight-forward (or even non-existent, as if that were possible), with the unfortunate implication that style for him is the servant of content and, therefore, not to be taken too seriously.[1] Yet, Moravia is a master of controlled narrative technique. While it is encouraging to note that a few critics have started to give long over-due attention to Moravia's style, the fact remains that the majority prefers to deal especially with the sociological content, the Marxism, the Freudianism, and in his last years the Moravian preoccupations with the twentieth-century's automatization and dehumanization of modern humankind.

In an interview with Mirella Serri in *La Stampa*, Moravia, himself, complains ironically that Italian critics focus *too much* on "i meriti formali," and that criticism "è fin troppo attenta alle questioni di stile." In general, however, focused textual analysis does not characterize Italian criticism which, on the contrary, has traditionally concentrated upon studying the psycho-socio-political angles of narration.

Among those exceptions to be noted especially for their perceptive textual analysis is Louis Kibler, who has written about Moravia's recurring images in "Imagery as Expression: Moravia's *Gli indifferenti*." Kibler pauses on the metaphor of the automobile, the mask, and on images such as rain and fog as they function symbolically within that novel. In addition, Gian Paolo Biasin draws some interesting parallels with Manzoni's Lucia in "Lucia secondo Moravia." Biasin takes into consideration Moravia's imagery of lambs and goats, with their premonitory and sacrificial functions;

---

[1] Sharon Wood provides a useful overview of the many critical dismissals of Alberto Moravia as a stylist, citing especially Olga Ragusa as having written: "his work which is traditional in structure and unimaginative in language will never benefit from the prestige-giving attention of 'close' reading" (Ragusa 141; see Wood 23-24).

however, he focuses less on the image itself than on how it describes Rosetta as a twentieth-century, Manzonian Lucia.

Jane Cottrell and Douglas Radcliff-Umstead have also paid some attention to his main images in their respective works, *Alberto Moravia* and "Moravia's Indifferent Puppets"; while Lucia Strappini in *Le cose e le figure negli Indifferenti* attempts to treat metaphor, but then deals mostly with abstract symbols (enclosed spaces, luminosity vs. darkness), rather than to consider specific imagery and instances of figurative language.

No critic to date has systematically examined any of the stylistic issues which cut across Moravia's complete works – issues which add immensely to our perception of how style in tandem with content offers a seamless statement of purpose to the reader. That final statement provides a congruence where every detail of the construct comes together to form an unshakable entity.

It is my intention to go substantially beyond the limited textual analyses that already have been done, and to offer a study of Moravia's imagery in his complete works to uncover as well some of what resides beneath Moravia's style. For literary criticism should offer more of a balance in its approaches to studying Moravia.

In this study I argue that his concerted and elaborate use of imagery not only enhances mimesis, but often provides a counterpoint to what he presents as objective "reality." (And there is no compelling evidence that Alberto Moravia conceived of narration as anything but mimetic. Indeed, Francesco Flora even rejoiced at Moravia's rejection of the tenets of Modernism remarking that he saw literature as "the correlative of something external to the text"; [see Wood, 3].)

Moravia relied heavily on imagery throughout his entire career, beginning in 1929 with *Gli indifferenti*, especially in his post-war publications after *La romana* (1947), and up to and including his last work, *La donna leopardo* (1991). As I. A. Richards has observed, " . . . we all live, and speak, only through our eye for resemblances. Without it we should perish early. Though some may have better eyes than others, the differences between them are in degree only and may be remedied" (48). Having an eye for the well-turned image is indeed a great asset for any writer, and this is especially so for Moravia.

Before proceeding, however, it would be well to establish a working definition of imagery as it is comprised specifically by its two major forms, metaphor and simile. In its simplest form, metaphor is a device used for describing one entity in terms of another unrelated one. The Greek term, *metapherein*, a transference of meaning, is composed of *meta,* over or beyond, and *pherein,* to carry. By carrying basic meaning beyond, metaphor modifies and alters that meaning, sometimes considerably. In a short statement, but freighted with significance, Paul Ricoeur states simply that "la métaphore est quelque chose qui arrive au nom" (23). ("Metaphor is something that happens to the noun" (Czerny 16).) Metaphor states that A *is* B – your eyes are the stars; your teeth are pearls.

Metaphor gives us a third way of seeing. It extends the meaning of what is being compared; it forces connections to be made. If A is linked to B, then the amalgam of A and B produces a third, C-entity which has the qualities of both A and B. When used consistently, metaphors can be tone givers; they can create yet a different, separate vision by suggesting the initial two entities for comparison. "Metaphor plugs the gaps in the literal vocabulary (or, at least, supplies the want of convenient abbreviations). So viewed, metaphor is a species of *catachresis*, which I shall define as the use of a word in some new sense in order to remedy a gap in the vocabulary. Catachresis is the putting of new senses into old words" (Black 280).

Simile, always closely linked with metaphor, also suggests new senses for old ways of seeing; it too offers interesting possibilities for previously unconsidered comparisons. Simile differs from metaphor in its explicit provision of the term, *like* or *as*, thus forcing the reader to consider the two previously incompatible concepts and to heed the possible ramifications of the comparison. Simile calls more attention to itself as a rhetorical device than metaphor does. Even dating back to Aristotle, students of imagery have noted that in simile the *relationship* is stressed while in metaphor the tenor's *being* the vehicle is stressed, with surprise playing a decisive role.[2]

---

[2] Ricoeur finds the best way to put it is that "l'élément commun à la métaphore et à la comparaison c'est l'assimilation qui fonde le transfert d'une dénomination, autrement dit, la saisie d'une identité dans la différence de deux termes. (. . .) Le transfert repose sur une ressemblance aperçue que la comparaison rend explicite par le moyen du terme de comparaison qui la caractérise. Que l'art génial de la métaphore consiste toujours dans une aperception des ressemblances est confirmé par le rapprochement avec la comparaison qui porte au langage la relation qui, dans la métaphore, est opérante sans être énoncée. La comparaison, dirons nous, exhibe le moment de ressemblance, opératoire mais non thématique, dans la métaphore" (38;

Simile provides its *like/as* in a clear, black and white print that simply cannot be ignored. George Miller thinks that, "What makes a simile striking, of course, is an author's sensitivity to previously unnoticed resemblances; it can link together two spheres of knowledge or experience in novel and revealing ways. In such cases, finding grounds for the comparison may be a nontrivial task. (. . .) Similes are less interesting than metaphors only in that the terms of the similitude are explicit and require less work from a reader. As far as interpretation is concerned, it is important to recognize that similes can pose all the apperceptive problems that metaphors can" (222). [3]

While a large body of contemporary work exists on the fine philosophical lines separating simile from metaphor (especially in recent years when philosophy has taken a linguistic turn), it is also generally agreed by modern rhetoricians that the main difference lies in the explicitness of the comparison, and that the other minor differences do not alter the importance of what they share. In this study, metaphor and simile will be considered together as figurative language, i.e., imagery. Indeed the broad contemporary consensus is compatible with Nelson Goodman who finds that "the difference between simile and metaphor is negligible" (77-78), and Christine Brooke-Rose who claims to rely on J. Middleton Murray's advice "to use 'image' for both simile and metaphor" (34). Abiding by their collective wisdom, in this study I will deliberately conflate the two basic definitions of simile and metaphor, forgoing the technical differences, to concentrate on the crucial similarities.

From Moravia's prose works (see Appendix B), I have attempted to cull all metaphors and similes that conform to the definitions

---

40). ("The element common to metaphor and simile is the assimilation that serves as foundation for the transfer of names. In other words, it is the apprehension of an identity within the difference between two terms. [. . .] The transfer rests on a perceived resemblance that simile makes explicit by means of its characteristic terms of comparison. The closeness of metaphor to simile brings to language the relationship that operates in metaphor without being articulated, and confirms that the inspired art of metaphor always consists in the apprehension of resemblances. We shall say that simile explicitly displays the moment of resemblance that operates implicitly in metaphor" [Czerny 26-27].)

[3] Simile is also generally considered a "less potent" image, while metaphor is defined by many as being more sophisticated, more complex in its allusiveness. "It follows, if my guess is anywhere near the truth, that a simile is usually less potent than a metaphor simply because (. . .) it is a *true* statement. It is not a provocation to correction, invention and discovery. We hear a metaphor and become a cat after a mouse. We pounce. A simile is more like a wheelbarrow – we are carried along" (Swanson 163).

as outlined above. (Your eyes are the stars/Your eyes are like the stars.) I have omitted what many today (especially in journalism) would call metaphors, but are in reality symbols and/or signs (such as a king's scepter, the international radioactivity warning indication, etc.). While metonymy and synechdoche are sometimes included in philosophical examinations of imagery, the most effective examples come to us from poetry. (See Eagleton 99.) Since very few clear examples of these devices appear in Moravia's prose works, I have chosen not to consider them in this study. I have also not considered "dead" metaphors and similes ("brutto come la fame," etc.) which have so entered into mainstream language that they effectively no longer carry imagistic meaning.

"Imagery" then throughout this study denotes any phrase clearly likening one entity to another, drawing a comparison, specific or implied. I have grouped in Appendix A all images with similar *tenors*, and then each is listed by the domain or realm of the *vehicle*. (In 1935 in his *The Philosophy of Rhetoric*, I. A. Richards established the terms *tenor* (the "real" meaning) and *vehicle* (the way of expressing it) to refer to the two parts of a comparison. In his often quoted Aristotelian example, "Achilles springs forth like a lion," Achilles is the tenor while the lion is the vehicle. These two terms have served almost every modern student of imagery since their original appearance.) It must be stressed that while there will always be exceptions, in this study I will be discussing generally the large categories and patterns into which Moravia's images fall.

It proved fruitless to separate the many images into positive and negative categories, because with very few exceptions, the images used to describe Moravia's characters are either negative, or they tend toward negativity and/or belittlement. Imagery to some degree cuts across all boundaries: men and women, sympathetic and antipathetic – all are Moravia's targets in one way or another. It seems not to matter what the character's role. The one categorical exception is that of the conceptual/existential images used for the male characters. Those are rarely explicitly negative (if at all); rather, they are neutrally descriptive, for the most part. Almost without exception, the imagery used to describe any individual's physical characteristics is judgmental, albeit vivid and sometimes even playful (as in Moravia's simile where a man's nose is likened to a pitcher handle). The vast majority of images not referring to humans is neutral or at least benign. This is to be expected; since one of imagery's primary purposes is to provide an enduring background picture for the reader to savor.[4] Imagistic neutrality most often occurs in non-human related similes and metaphors, a neutrality which is almost never the case when human characters enter into the picture.

Figurative language has an overarching importance in Moravia's prose style in all of his works. When taken to its extremes, well-orchestrated imagery becomes indispensable (such as that found in *La ciociara*; see Chapter V); it describes physically and psychologically; it blends and situates characters in a sort of interface of images; and it often provides important stylistic reinforcement to the major themes. In addition to its immediate descriptive function in other works, imagery can have what Wellek and Warren call a "subtler form of literary meaning" (188). In almost all cases, as a result of well-planned imagery, the reader acquires a richer perspective on the characters, a new, third way of seeing them.

Moravia's own view of imagery's uses can be extrapolated from what his characters have to say about it. Often they will tell the reader outright that they are going to use a metaphor or simile to help, for example, describe the indescribable within the confines of their own view of what "reality" is. (Yet, they never mention all the other stylistic devices that they could also choose to help express themselves.) Clearly metaphor and simile are Moravia's (and their) favorite way to describe. The characters alert the reader to the stylistic potential of imagery and the highly visual nature of discourse.

In *Il conformista* Marcello describes his *simpatia* for Franco. "Per simpatia, insomma, dando a questa parola un senso tutto irriflesso, alogico, irrazionale. Una simpatia che si poteva dire soltanto per metafora che veniva dall'aria; ma in aria ci sono il polline dei fiori, i fumi delle case, la polvere, la luce, non le idee" (93). Implicitly Marcello knows that his only means of expression for the *simpatia* he feels is indeed through metaphor as a kind of last resort, imperfect as that means may be. Marcello denigrates metaphor by apologizing for using a device as ubiquitous as dust, smoke and pollen, but one without the importance of true ideas.

In some instances Moravia's character will resort to using imagery when words fail him; and he will warn the reader of what he

---

[4] Bruno Quaranta thinks that metaphor alone can even "conferire allo stile una specie di longevità."

is about to do. "Per adoperare una metafora, la realtà, quando mi annoio, mi ha sempre fatto l'effetto sconcertante che fa una coperta troppo corta, ad un dormiente, in una notte d'inverno: la tira sui piedi e ha freddo al petto, la tira sul petto e ha freddo ai piedi; e così non riesce mai a prender sonno veramente" (*La noia* 7). Later the same character finds again that plain language fails him: " . . . mi limiterò ad alludervi con una metafora . . ." (19). Much like Marcello's apology, his implicit requests for forgiveness again point up the perception of imagery as a second class rhetorical device.

Not so implicit, however, is a case in *L'attenzione*. In a rather Pirandellian layering of different fictive realities, an instance of self-parody occurs where the narrator, a would-be author, sees a rotting sheep's carcass on the beach and compares it to his wife, but decides that in "his novel" he will not use that metaphor because "mi sono detto che sarebbe stato un effetto pessimo, come di cosa vecchia e di cattivo gusto, quale può venire in mente ad uno scrittore mediocre e antiquato" (161-62). In Moravia's third last work, *Il viaggio a Roma*, the protagonist says, "Scusami sono costretto ancora una volta a servirmi della metafora, ma è indispensabile" (49).

Imagery is considered imperfect, something for which the narrator begs the reader's pardon; yet, it is always employed when "real" language is found lacking. It helps to convey messages through a kind of desperate symbolic code. While keeping in mind what we have learned from recent post-deconstruction discourse about the nature of "slippery reality" (especially with the current emphasis on Lacanian interpretations of blurring of meaning), here and throughout this study I will, nevertheless, respect Moravia's attempt to "provisionally nail down words onto meaning" (see Eagleton 169) without regard to the evident post-modern impossibility of ever really succeeding. After all, it is Moravia himself who, in *L'attenzione* (299), refers to the tenor of a metaphor as "il vero nome".

Metaphoric language substitutes for *il vero nome* in *L'attenzione* where the protagonist, speaking of his wife's second job of being a procuress at a so-called *sartoria*, calls the tenor of his metaphor *il vero nome*, making the vehicle a *parola paravento*: "Ancora una volta, oggi, andando a spasso per il quartiere, mi sono posto la domanda: "perché, parlando con Cora, hai ricorso alla metafora della sartoria, invece di chiamare con il vero nome il suo secondo mestiere? perché, insomma, non sei capace di affrontare francamente e direttamente la questione più importante della tua vita?" (299).

Metaphor, in this instance, is not just another way of seeing, but sometimes a cleaner, easier way of dealing with a dirty, less comfortable reality (elusive as that "reality" may be).

In the short story, "Al dio ignoto," the female protagonist, a rather unconventional nurse to say the least, masturbates her patients, but leaves the sheet as a covering to keep her *dio ignoto* a veiled mystery. "Ho visto per la prima volta quegli sfioramenti come qualche cosa di vizioso. E allora ho deciso di tirare via il lenzuolo. Ho esclamato un po' ironico: 'Che cos'è? Una metafora? Parli per simboli?'" (*La cosa* 42). Metaphor thus transmits messages symbolically. It is a remedy for when something's true name (*il vero nome*) for some reason cannot be uttered; the image becomes a euphemism, a poetic evasion of "reality." Imagery sometimes functions as does allegory, telling a story, relating an incident, or making a point in a different way, by speaking of other things (to adopt the precise meaning of allegory) – things different from the literal target. Imagery is the only recourse when plain language no longer suffices, even if it means being a "scrittore mediocre e antiquato." In a very real sense, it is an example of catachresis, where its use gives fresh meaning to overly used concepts.

As mentioned briefly above, I. A. Richards separates the two elements of an image with the terms *tenor* and *vehicle*. The former is the concept to which a second idea is linked. So when Moravia says that a house of prostitution is a *sartoria*, the house (*il vero nome*) is the tenor; the *sartoria* is the vehicle. These designations as well can be useful in this study; "for the whole task is to compare the different relations which, in different cases, these two members of a metaphor hold to one another (Richards 52). Again, a third idea emerges from the union of two disparate ones: ". . . in many of the most important uses of metaphor, the co-presence of the vehicle and tenor results in a meaning (to be clearly distinguished from the tenor) which is not attainable without their interaction. That vehicle is not normally a mere embellishment of a tenor which is otherwise unchanged by it but that vehicle and tenor in co-operation give a meaning of more varied powers than can be ascribed to either" (Richards 55).

The protagonist in *L'uomo che guarda* resorts to the metaphor in a pair of instances. First he compares a conversation with his father to taking short cuts while driving a car, and later he deliberately searches for the proper related metaphor. "Mio padre parla tra i denti, con impazienza, dietro il giornale. E' chiaro che desidera che mi tolga al più presto dai piedi. Allora, spinto dall'urgenza, tanto per continuare la metafora, invece di uscire dall'autostrada per lo svincolo, semplicemente salto il guardrail: 'Papà, poco fa, non ti ho detto la verità, non è del problema atomico che volevo parlarti, ma di qualche cosa di personale, di privato. (. . .) Cerco una metafora e alla fine dico con più estro che convinzione: Ulisse si fa legare all'albero della nave e otturare le orecchie con la cera per non sentire il canto delle sirene' " (88; 95). The extended metaphor is the only way for the character to convey the non-mincing bluntness and urgency of his conversation with his father, his sentences careening out, indeed like a car jumping the rail, rather than exiting his metaphorical freeway in a logical, linear way.

Another useful Moravian explanation of the function of imagery appears again in *L'attenzione*. The narrator discusses briefly catachresis, the idea of attributing new meaning through imagery, of forcing a rapport between the tenor and its vehicle, and the danger of "reality" becoming less than "real." "Ma al tempo stesso, in maniera contraddittoria, tu non puoi fare a meno di attribuire dei significati alle cose e agli eventi, di trasformare le persone in simboli, di ordinare e mettere in rapporto significati e simboli secondo schemi ideologici. E così, invincibilmente, Baba, Cora, te stesso e quello che tu hai fatto o meglio non hai fatto e quello che Cora ha fatto a Baba e quello che Baba ha subito si caricano nella tua mente di significati, si trasformano in metafore, sono sempre in pericolo di perdere il loro peso e il loro spessore di realtà e di diventare parti intercambiabili di un solo discorso astratto" (164).

On this higher level, imagery has the power to put abstract distance between "objective reality" and our perceptions of what is "real." Moravia's extensive use of these devices over the years has done more than that – not so much as imagery functions traditionally as a tool of his style, but as it systematically bends, twists, splices, blurs and modifies the reader's expectations of certain characters throughout his *opera omnia*.

Especially interesting about Moravia's works of fiction (in all some 45 novels and collections) is the stylistic phenomenon of *image-ization*, a term coined for this study to refer to the cumulative effect of large numbers of kindred metaphors and similes dedicated to men and women in general, to groups of people, to whole sectors of society, objects, and thoughts. For Moravia relies on imagery to inform his prose to an almost unparalleled extent in modern Italian fiction.[5]

Throughout his complete works there abound:

(a) images that are clearly and simply there for richness of description, used in all of the conventional ways to describe and to enhance the prose narrative;

(b) images that are seemingly discrete (i.e., not part of a literary continuum or a master plan), but in fact upon close examination do not appear to be random at all. At times they evince certain tendencies that in subtle ways help to advance some of Moravia's basic themes. When organized they show interesting things about attitudes, stereotypes and prejudices, whether they are provided purposefully to characterize the fictive actors or are a symptom relating to perceptions just below the consciousness of the author;

(c) images whose use is associative and which have been obviously and sophisticatedly implanted with some degree of structural complexity by the author to help advance the plot in rudimentary ways. For example, in his short story, "Un dritto," Moravia tells us that if a one-kilo loaf of bread could have an expression of sadness, that would be the face of the protagonist's wife.[6] With clever manipulation of this image, by the end of the short story the wife is a loaf of bread in the reader's perception. The narrator then declares that the wayward husband does not like homemade bread any longer. Moravia uses a specific image to describe the wife, and then makes that controlling image the pivotal one of the story; and

(d) imagery so orchestrated that it governs the narrative's main theme, as metaphors and similes do in *La ciociara,* for example, where they play a full and dynamic role in the narrative architecture of the novel.[7]

---

[5] Vasco Pratolini is the only other Italian novelist who even approaches Moravia's extended use of metaphor as an informing principle; yet, metaphor figures significantly in only two of his novels. See Janice M. Kozma, "Metaphor in Pratolini's Novels: *Il quartiere* and *Cronache di poveri amanti," Romance Notes* 20.3 (1980): 1-6; Janice M. Kozma, "Functions of Metaphor in Pratolini's *Cronache di poveri amanti*: Maciste and the Signora," *Italian Culture* 3 (1981): 87-102; and Janice M. Kozma, "Pratolini's *Il quartiere*: The Metaphor," *Kentucky Romance Quarterly* 29.1 (1982): 37-45.

[6] ". . . e se una pagnotta di un chilo potesse avere una espressione di tristezza, ebbene avrebbe quella che subito notai sul viso ottuso e massiccio di Agnese" (Moravia, "Un dritto," *Nuovi racconti romani* 93).

[7] For a detailed analysis see Jan Kozma-Southall, "Omen and Image: Presage and Sacrifice in Moravia's *La ciociara," Italica* 61.3 (1984): 207-19.

In what follows I take up each of the four categories. I deal with imagery both (a) in subtext (chapters II and III), as it separates from its primary role and assumes a different, intertextual function, and (b) in context (chapters IV and V), as it is amalgamated to the storyline and is assigned an associative purpose. While my main purpose here is to explore Moravia's stylistic design, I do not ignore the random image, and thus begin with those.

I I

DISCRETE IMAGERY

Metaphor is a tool so ordinary that we use it uncon-
sciously and automatically, with so little effort that we
hardly notice it. It is omni-present: metaphor suffuses
our thoughts, no matter what we are thinking about. It
is accessible to everyone: as children, we automatically,
as a matter of course, acquire a mastery of everyday
metaphor. It is conventional: metaphor is an integral
part of our ordinary everyday thought and language.
And it is irreplaceable: metaphor allows us to understand our selves and our world in ways that no other
modes of thought can."

(Lakoff and Turner, xi)

Moravia's use of imagery cuts across all the different periods
of his career. From *Gli indifferenti* to his last work, *La donna leopardo,* metaphors and similes of all types can be identified – about 850
different images appear in Moravia's *opera omnia.* [1] Some are used
over and over again, bringing the total number of metaphors and
similes to well over 1750. Moravia is masterful at creating a sustained narrative structure out of those images; and in many cases
that architecture of imagery supports literally certain key elements

---

[1] While I have made every effort to collect and count each metaphor and simile,
it is not my intention to offer elaborate statistics or to claim to have absolutely precise numerical data. In a study of this kind, there will always be instances where one
particular image may have been overlooked or perhaps counted twice. My purpose
is to be accurate enough, however, to present a balanced picture of what occurs
with metaphor and simile in Moravia's complete works. My intention is to offer am-
ply and clearly documented examples which represent the general trends of imagery in Moravia's complete works.

of the plot (see especially Chapter V). On a more creatively simple level, however, Moravia is also capable of turning the most felicitous phrases, perhaps not always with important thematic ramifications, but with great imagistic flair.

Images not referring to specific individuals, for the most part, are used in the conventional ways of narration; i.e., to enrich the prose through description, and to enable the reader to conceptualize the descriptions more fully through pictures. "Because metaphors allow us to describe features of our world that lie beyond our direct experience, they have the capacity to expand the scope, range, relevancy, accuracy and applicability of a perspective. Their non-literal comparisons allow us to break imaginative boundaries and to express the heuristic power of thought. We invent metaphors when we find literal language too dull, restrictive, or inaccurate" (Deshler 24).

A whole spectrum of images not pertaining to named men and women includes several categories:

(a) *Abstract Imagery*: reality is a Chinese box, for example, in *Il disprezzo*. "Come nelle scatole cinesi, ciascuna delle quali ne contiene una più piccola, la realtà pareva contenere un sogno il quale a sua volta conteneva una realtà che a sua volta conteneva ancora un sogno e così all'infinito" (255).[2] Imagery can represent truth, which in one instance reveals itself as a Venus flytrap. "Kleist! Piano, piano al suono di quel nome, la verità si dischiudeva sotto i miei occhi, come uno di quei malsani fiori carnivori dei tropici i quali aprono i petali soltanto per afferrare qualche insetto che poi, a petali chiusi, divoreranno lentamente" (*1934* 69).

(b) *Imagery of Thought*: thoughts can be nuts in an empty bag (*NRR,* "La verità" 431); a rush of thoughts might be equated with agitated birds in a cage (*La romana* 288); an incipient thought is a bird on a windowsill (*RR,* "La rovina dell'umanità" 203).

(c) *Images of Ennui*: where, for example, *noia* is transformed into an interruption of electricity. "Oppure, altro paragone, la mia noia rassomiglia all'interruzione frequente e misteriosa della corrente elettrica in una casa: un momento tutto è chiaro ed evidente, qui sono le poltrone, lì i divani, più in là gli armadi, le console, i

---

[2] The same "Chinese Box" image appears as well in Moravia's essay, "L'uomo come fine" (172).

quadri, i tendaggi, i tappeti, le finestre, le porte; un momento dopo non c'è più che buio e vuoto" (*La noia* 7).[3]

(d) *Erotic Images*: such as the extended one describing Cora's opening a bottle of champagne:

> Cora, dunque, prende tra le mani bianche, lisce e impure la bottiglia massiccia di vetro scuro, dell'etichetta gialla, dal collo avvolto in stagnola rossa; e tenendola un poco lontano da sè, la sigaretta stretta all'angolo della bocca e gli occhi socchiusi, sospinge in su, con il pollice, il grosso tappo legato con un filo di ferro intrecciato. Il pollice candido dall'unghia ovale, convessa e scarlatta, fa uscire pian piano il tappo dal collo della bottiglia, poi avviene la rituale esplosione. (. . .) Io non posso fare a meno, guardando la mano di Cora che si abbarbica sul vetro nero della bottiglia con le dita lunghe e bianche, e al fiotto schiumoso che a scosse ripetute e successive, erompe nei bicchieri; non posso fare a meno, dico, di pensare che a quello stesso modo, nella casa di Cora, al momento dell'orgasmo, erompe, dopo una lunga preparazione, il seme maschile. (*L'attenzione* 83)

(e) *Concrete Images:* where *anagrafe* bureaucrats are "anime in pena" (*NRR,* "La raccomandazione" 16); where a hot Roman summer day is "come se tutta Roma fosse stata un solo bucato di panni sporchi," and where the flagstones of a street are *pagnotte* (*NRR,* "La vita leggera" 247).

(f) *Imagery from the Natural World*: " . . . le nuvole dorate di sole e orlate di grigio che si muovevano, secondo il vento, come gli intestini di un ventre in subbuglio" (*Una cosa è una cosa,* "L'albero di Giuda" 344), and where a boat's wake of water becomes "un merletto bianco ed evanescente sulla seta cangiante del mare" (*L'automa,* "L'evasione" 22).

(g) *Animal/Insect Imagery*: In *Nuovi racconti romani,* "Lo scimpanzè," the chimpanzees' rumps are likened to "un mazzo di melanzane violette," whereas another is eating a banana "come una persona" (34).

---

[3] For an interesting discussion of Moravia's own experience with *la noia*, see Moravia and Elkann. "È una forma di angoscia che mi è congenita e che via via nei miei libri ho chiamato noia, disperazione, mancanza di rapporto con la realtà, incapacità di azione ecc. Dico congenita perchè ricordo di avere sofferto di questa angoscia anche da bambino quando letteralmente, come ho detto, non avevo alcuna esperienza della vita. Probabilmente questa cosiddetta noia è l'altra faccia di una sensibilità eccessiva e perciò facilmente delusa" (282).

(h) *Food Imagery*: where onions are swords, and Savoy cabbage (*verze*) is equated with a baby's head (*RR*, "Il tesoro" 346).

(i) *Machine Imagery*: where a long line of cars is transformed into "la mandria ferma" (*Il paradiso*, "Noiosi" 146).

(j) *Imagery of Architecture*: an apartment building is a dog-pound and its balconies are like soapholders (*RR*, "Il naso" 371); where throughout Moravia's works bedrooms are wombs, and corridors are intestines often reflecting the nature of twentieth-century life as it forces man to wend his way through serpentine hallways and mazes.

(k) *Images of the Human Body* (not in relation to any specific male and female characters): where a man's face is likened to the skin of a late-maturing orange (*La romana* 455), and a man's nose is a *gnocco* or a bell-clapper (*RR* 370) or a pitcher handle (*RR* 40).

(l) *Imagery of War*: mostly in *La ciociara*, again and again Nazis in general are savage beasts, poisonous snakes, tigers and wolves. The *sfollati* are plants uprooted and transplanted into alien soil. Starving civilians, all stooped over picking cicory weed for survival, are "anime in Purgatorio."

Upon close examination of all the images in Moravia's complete works, it appears that those referring to most *inanimate* objects and concepts are randomly there for the usual reasons of colorful description, background enhancements, etc., as they "donnent un 'vêtement' à l'expression nue de la pensée" (Ricoeur 66). (As they "cloth(e) the naked expression of thought" (Czerny 46).)

Not much beyond that fact can or should be inferred from their appearance, since the numbers of images within their patterns are not especially overwhelming, and there seems to be no compelling evidence of any other reason for their existence, save for playful description. They can for the most part be considered as curious cultural artifacts.

Aristotle, speaking about the instructive value of metaphor says, "This quality really concerns the pleasure of understanding that follows surprise. For this is the function of metaphor, to instruct by suddenly combining elements that have not been put together before." Ricoeur cites Aristotle as well, "We all naturally find it agreeable to get hold of new ideas easily: words express ideas, and therefore those words are the most agreeable that enable us to get hold of new ideas. Now strange words simply puzzle us; ordinary words convey only what we know already; it is from metaphor that we can best get hold of something fresh" (Rhetoric 1410b 10-15).

What ultimate function does one well-turned image have, save to enhance our appreciation of any given scene, and perhaps let us "get hold of something fresh"? In most cases, none. When we read that a Polariod photo emerging from a camera is a tongue sticking out, how is the actual action of the plot moved along, for example, or how do we gain insight into the complex workings of the mind? Perhaps not a whole lot; yet, without those finely constructed "morceaux brillants," the prose and the reader's experience would be poorer.

Yet some interesting patterns do reveal themselves when one plays with all the various images in this category. For example, when they function as tenor, the many abstractions of the human thought process share a vehicular predilection for nature and the cosmos. Mental abstractions, thought and boredom are equated with monsters, wild beasts, caged beasts, rivers, termites, plants, trees, vegetables, puppies, serpents, wild horses, Venus flytraps, horseflies, caged birds, sidereal spaces, clouds, cyclones, whirlwinds, fog, and a marine vortex. Furthermore, taking a quick look at Appendix A, under the rubric of Abstract Imagery it is evident that we are not dealing with a very kindly mother nature, but with a preponderance of sometimes violent and scary images used to describe the life of the mind.

The use of imagery is not just the substitution of one idea for another; something new is introduced involving additional information to be added to the original concept, idea, thing. If not, as Ricoeur states, "la métaphore n'a qu'une valeur ornementale, décorative" (30); "la métaphore porte une information, parce qu'elle 're-décrit' la réalité" (32). ("Then metaphor has only an ornamental, decorative value," (20), but "metaphor bears information because it redescribes reality" [Czerny 22].) So what is Moravia telling his readers when his most frequently used images implicitly inform us that violence and fright, force and fury are the cumulative equivalence of our aggregate mental abstractions, thought and spiritual ennui? Is he using (even if unwittingly) the accrued stylistic effect of random imagery throughout his works to second his often primary theme of human alienation and existential despair?

It is logical that images of war would feature violence and upheaval – where Nazis and Fascists are beasts, snakes, wolves and insects, where the refugees are uprooted plants and unprotected animals, where weapons are equated with every destructive image imaginable from ugly animals to bloody razor slits, and where the Allies are saints. But why are precisely the images of mental activity too often so closely related to havoc and fury? What does it mean in Moravia's world to think, to cogitate? For, clearly in his prose contemplation is not a happy, positive activity; it is at least as bad as war in its metaphorical representation.

In *Le Bruissement de la Langue*, Roland Barthes talks about the traditionally aesthetic function of pure description in his essay, "L'effet du réel" (170). He talks about western civilization's fascination with ekphrasis, the "morceau brillant, détachable (ayant donc sa fin en soi, indépendante de toute fonction d'ensemble)" even going back to the 2nd century AD. He cites Curtius (see his Chapter X) who says that description in those times had nothing to do with realism, description was not referential. Then Barthes takes a great leap to *Madame Bovary* and traces that descriptive tradition to Flaubert's description of Rouen which he finds "parfaitement impertinente par rapport à la structure narrative de Madame Bovary" (171).

Taking a Barthesean jump from the late 19th century to Alberto Moravia's contemporary works, it might be agreed that as in *Madame Bovary* a great deal of his descriptive imagery is "impertinente," and even perhaps could be deleted without doing great damage to the emplotment and general narrative structure. Yet, on the other hand, what are we as readers to make of imagery that equates the modern thought process in less than positive ways, that can be interpreted as generally frightening (monsters, beasts, fogs), confining (caged birds), destructive (termites, serpents, horseflies, Venus flytrap) and out of control (rivers, wild beasts, wild horses, cyclones, whirlwinds, vortices)? Barthes argues that by means of the ensemble of all these details "il se produit un effet du réel, fondement de ce vraisemblable ma voué qui forme l'esthétique de toutes les oeuvres courantes de la modernité" (174).

Similarly when we examine the imagery connected with concrete "reality," the natural/physical world, architecture, machines, eroticism, human body parts and food, to a certain degree the vehicles in these categories also indicate a decided tendency toward insects, animals and plants, but there is not the same concentrated suggestion of negativity. Since the tenors themselves are so random and different from each other, the effect is greatly diffused, not at all what it is with abstractions of thought where there is a clear connection between the very real existence of the mind and imagistic unpleasantries. If my reading of this collective imagery is correct, it could be the case that Moravia's works contain a certain hidden agenda, a subtext which on another level underscores the existential themes in Moravia's prose, an undercurrent which forms much more of a total didactic program than has been examined to date.

The above discussion pertains to those images *not* connected to men and women, to imagery where the tenor is for the most part not human (or, in the case of Nazis, Fascists, etc., not functioning primarily as humans, but as ciphers for an entire socio-political entity). The above, however, is also true in the case of those metaphors and similes which *do* pertain to the main characters in Moravia's prose. By virtue of their sheer numbers and convincing patterns in all of Moravia's works, however, those human-related metaphors and similes present in addition certain other problems that call for much closer scrutiny.

While numbers alone can never persuade in literary studies, just a glance at a few elementary numerical facts provokes some interesting questions: of those over 1750 images (of which about 850 are different similes and metaphors) appearing throughout Moravia's complete works, about 1450 of them refer to men and women (i.e., over 80 %). In *Il paradiso*, "Angelo mio," a mother affectionately addresses her son, " . . . tesoro, amore, cuoricino, topino, gioia, bambino, gattino, luce dei miei occhi, creaturina, omettino, passerotto, anatroccolo, trombolino, frugoletto, angelo . . ." (13). While this avalanche of epithets targeted at only one individual is hardly the norm in Moravia's use of imagery, the wide gamut of different images devoted to his characters is truly impressive and indeed emblematic of his predilection for the device.

Imagery of people as animals is by far the largest category for both women and men, there being well over 700 instances. The next largest group concerns the body parts of men and women which appear about 160 times. Men and women appear as food about 60 times, and as masks, machines, plants, flowers and miscellaneous gadgetry about 400 times. These convincing numbers alert the careful reader to explore further that subtext of concentrations of images, clusterings of concepts, and density of kindred ideas.

III

SEEMINGLY DISCRETE IMAGERY

> Aggiungo: un'idea di balbuziente che, nell'impossi-
> bilità di comunicare con la parola, ricorre al lin-
> guaggio figurato, metaforico: adesso fermerò la
> donna e mi servirò di lei come di un segno simboli-
> co per trasmettere un messaggio al sistema nemico
> che mi vuole rapito e ucciso.
>
> ("Ho balbettato tutta la mia vita," *La cosa* 212)

In this chapter I examine those images pertaining to women
and men that are seemingly discrete, not part of an orchestrated literary effort within the limits of just one work. I hope to demon-
strate that in the majority of instances their random quality is really
not so random at all, and that throughout his complete works
Moravia's metaphors and similes fall into many widely represented
categories that shed light upon his thought process, his attitudes
and his broad thematics in some very interesting and perhaps even
surprising ways.

On the most basic, functional level, all of Moravia's images are
appropriate to the specific context in which they appear; they are
never gratuitous. The images pertain directly to the characters
whom they describe; very few images (if any) are unconnected to
the scenes which they enhance.

There is another important level, however, at which one can le-
gitimately look at an author's image choices, and that is the level at
which they fall into general patterns and categories, quite aside
from the above, i.e., from whatever their primary function might be
within the text. Seen as such, these images elucidate Moravia's
thought process and his mimetic imagination in surprising ways;

for, when examined *sui generis* they are momentarily divorced from the characters whom they describe. Patterns emerge more clearly. The images form a corpus when they leave that basic, principal context and become intermixed, organized and examined as a rhetorical entity unto itself. Seen schematically, the resulting classifications into which the images cohere bring to light unexpected implications, inferences which also clarify the author's views on women and men and their relationships to one another in ways that have not been fully appreciated.

In literary criticism sheer quantity of examples alone cannot be invoked as evidence; statistical play and data massage are not the purposes of this inquiry. Yet, it is nevertheless significant that of the approximately 1450 images devoted to men and women, some 850 of them refer to women alone; i.e., a significantly larger percentage (+/− 60%) of the total human-related metaphors and similes is devoted to women. Further, women occupy some special categories all to themselves: they are statues, madonnas, babies, dolls, objects of property, and not insignificantly, death (about 185 images in just these categories).

The only category mostly represented by men is that of conceptual imagery. Over 20 times (vs. only 4 clear examples for women) men are likened at length in extended images to existential concepts which help to describe the way a man's mind works. For example, a man's confused brain is described as an explosion in a china shop (*L'attenzione* 119). When a man adopts a fetal position because of an existential crisis which he seems to be experiencing, he is presented as a wad of clothing in an automatic washing machine seen through the porthole (*Una cosa è una cosa* 278). When a man sees a nude woman, his thoughts fly away like a flock of sparrows leaving a tree when a gun is shot through it (*La ciociara* 166). Imagery abounds in which the life of a man's mind is equated with various objects: boats, flames, icebergs, soap bubbles, digital numbers, candles, just to name a few. The life of a woman's mind gets no such attention (to be sure, in most Moravian cases, she does not even have one).

Close analysis of all these "random" images uncovers some surprising configurations when they are all collected into similar groups. The metaphors and similes start to lose their scattered quality, and begin to take on the patterning characteristics of orchestrated threads carefully woven into the thematic mesh of Moravia's narrative. While both men and women are compared to animals, food items, puppets, masks,[1] machines, and their body parts are a whole gamut of objects and concepts, women are more consistently and extensively image-ized into categories than are men. There are more metaphors and similes of women than there are of men in almost all shared categories. Further, women alone are singled out as being:

(a) STATUES AND MADONNAS: For example, in Moravia's short story, "Il seduttore," we read: "Avevo notato da un pezzo questa ragazza bella come una statua, immobile come una statua, fredda come una statua e, incoraggiato dal fatto che sembrava una statua, e le statue, si sa, non rispondono ma anche non si offendono, le avevo detto: 'Bellezza . . .' Lei a queste parole, da vera statua . . ." (*NRR* 556). Madonna imagery abounds in *L'uomo che guarda,* where in this one instance the wife concedes: "Via, non essere così triste. Dopo tutto è meglio essere trattata come una madonna che come una vacca" (117). There is no choice for the wife other than madonna or cow. (Ironically she is having sexual relations on the side with her father-in-law who likes to call her a *porca,* completing the full circle and making her the very embodiment of the expletive, *porca-madonna.*)[2]

(b) DOLLS AND BABIES: In "Felice," we meet one of many Moravian women "con un volto di bambola" (*Un'altra vita* 126). Patrizia

---

[1] Douglas Radcliff-Umstead treats Moravia's use of puppet and mask imagery in his perceptive article, "Moravia's Indifferent Puppets." Along the same lines Cottrell in *Alberto Moravia* remarks: "Masks naturally hide the self, and they are of prime importance in Moravia's early works. (. . .) Its function is to hide the self from the self. Hypocrisy is the companion to a mask, and is the predominant sin of the middle class of Moravia, who delights in unmasking the masked and exposing hypocrisy of his readers. A mask may be consciously adopted by a Moravian character as a calculated method of getting along in life" (29). *Maschera* in Italian means both mask and make-up, and often links the two in their double meaning. Make-up for Moravia almost never has its usual function of enhancing a woman's face. In his works it mostly exaggerates her negative qualities instead.

[2] "First, what is it about the representation of the Maternal in general, and about the Christian or virginal representation in particular, that enables it not only to calm social anxiety and supply what the male lacks, but also to satisfy a woman, in such a way that the community of the sexes is established beyond, and in spite of, their flagrant incompatibility and permanent state of war? Second, what is it about this representation that fails to take account of what a woman might say or want of the Maternal, so that when today women make their voices heard, the issues of conception and maternity are a major focus of discontent? Such protests go beyond sociopolitical issues and raise "civilization's discontents" to such a pitch that even Freud recoiled at the prospect: the discontent is somehow in the species itself." See Julia Kristeva, "Stabat Mater," *The Kristeva Reader* (163).

of *Io e lui* is "bruna, il volto vezzoso e perfetto smaltato di rosa, come una bambola di porcellana o una madonna di cera" (295). (In his second last work, *La villa del venerdì*, in the short story entitled, "Sull'autostrada," the protagonist offers a woman a gift; of all the gifts she could choose, she opts for a doll.) The *Nuovi racconti romani* collection even features a whole story entitled precisely "Bambolona," while the collection, *Boh!*, provides the following passage pointing up the degree to which random metaphor may be extended:

> A Madrid, scendiamo in un albergo di lusso; quindi passiamo tutto il pomeriggio del primo giorno andando da un negozio all'altro per ricostituire il mio guardaroba. E' come giocare con una di quelle bambole moderne, che si vendono nude coi vestiti a parte, e le bambine si divertono a rivestirle, cominciando dallo slip fino alla camicetta e alla gonna. La bambola sono io, nuda sotto il mio soprabito; e rivestirmi per il mio compagno è un gioco erotico perché è innamorato e si diverte a spendere per me e a me fa piacere che si diverta in questo modo . . . il pomeriggio vola, leggero, allegro, tenero e scherzoso, proprio come se giocassimo ambedue con questa bambola da rivestire dalla testa ai piedi che è il mio corpo. (108)

This living, breathing "Barbie Doll" is so accustomed to playing the role for her lover that she is comfortable referring to herself as she would to a third party – a doll to be dressed and preened.

While it is (unfortunately) conventional in our culture that madonnas, dolls, babies, and the like refer to women, the fact is that Moravia consciously chose and created these similes and metaphors; as an alternative, he could have chosen not to image-ize the women at all. Male characters have no direct counterparts to these images. Men do not appear as "GI Joe" children's toys or as chest-beating action figures, which perhaps would serve as the equivalents to dolls and babies, if Moravia had wanted to present them as such.

(c) OBJECTS OF PROPERTY: In the play, *La vita è gioco,* Remigio and Berengario are contracting to transfer ownership of a young prostitute, Nirvana. When she asks to sign the contract as well, Remigio informs her, "Che c'entri tu? Mica quando si fa il contratto per la vendita di una vitella, si fa firmare la vitella." But Nirvana quickly answers, "La vitella non sa scrivere, io sì" (26). In spirit much like the "Barbie Doll" in *Boh!*, Nirvana considers herself no more than a *literate* heifer (but still a heifer, nevertheless).

A discussion of women as objects would be incomplete without considering a passage from *La vita interiore* where the protagonist's mother, a madame, peddles her daughter's virginity over the telephone to an especialy exigent customer:

> Voglio dire che non è del tipo (. . .) andante, che si trova dapperttutto, è invece qualche cosa di fine, di eccezionale. (. . .) Si tratta (. . .) di un oggetto di valore, non soltanto perché è nuovo, cioè appena uscito dalla fabbrica, ma anche perché non è fabbricato in serie, ma per modo di dire, a mano, un esemplare alla volta. (. . .) Che dice, non si fida? Ma come devo dirglielo che è una merce sicura, garantita nuova di zecca, di quelle che i commercianti tengono da parte per i loro clienti più importanti. Se c'è pericolo? E quale pericolo? Non è mica roba di contrabbando, l'ho avuta in perfetta regola, spontaneamente, liberamente. E' vero, è un prodotto uscito dalla fabbrica sì e no una dozzina di anni fa, un prodotto non ancora collaudato, ma lei può star sicuro che funziona a meraviglia. Lei ce l'avrà a completa disposizione, potrà farne quello che vuole, magari anche romperlo, poi se ne va a casa e al resto ci penso io. Sì, romperlo, dopo tutto è roba sua, lei lo paga e ha tutto il diritto di fare quello che vuole, senza rendere conto a nessuno. (65-66)

The mother's long equation of her daughter's virgin body as new merchandise is replete with all the appropriate technical vocabulary forming one of the most extended metaphors in Moravia's works. While it is obvious to any reader that on one level this whole conversation is deliberately carried out in code to avoid the appearance of dealing in prostitution, nevertheless the scene could have been reported in some other way to avoid the extended metaphor, if the author had opted to do so.

The same occurs in *L'attenzione* where Cora, the procuress, has her own telephonic argot whereby her girls are combs: "pettini di tartaruga bionda o bruna, per far capire che la ragazza è bionda o bruna. Poi dice che questi pettini hanno sedici, diciotto, venti o venticinque denti. Sono gli anni della ragazza." If the girl is a virgin, then she is a "tipo nuovo, mai visto" (122). In tone and function, these passages are very similar to the Nirvana and Barbie examples where the female character is first metaphorically dehumanized and then accepted as being such to the point where her original identity is suppressed and forgotten.

(d) FLOWERS AND PLANTS: In "Bassetto" Marcella is "proprio una rosa" (*RR* 358), while in *Il conformista* Giulia's body is "il fusto di una pianta appassita" (207). In "L'amicizia" the female protagonist's big face is one of those "rose che si chiamano cavolone appunto perché sono fitte e grosse come cavoli" (*RR* 194). The protagonist of a story in *Il paradiso*, "I prodotti," describes herself: "(I)o ero destinata a diventare una donna formosa; e poi, come avviene alle piante se non sono spesso innaffiate, mi era mancata la linfa, cioè la vitalità" (193). *La romana* sees her own beauty as "una rosa in una ragnatela" (378).

and (e) DEATH: A bizarre example from *L'attenzione* features an interesting dialogue where it is simply a "given" that the man and woman are in harmonious agreement on the woman's being death personified:

> 'Perché quel tedesco ti trattava da scheletro, ti chiamava morte.'
> (. . .) 'Va bene, sono la morte: e con questo? Vieni, su, facciamo
> l'amore.' (. . .) Sì, pensai, lei era la morte, quella delle danze
> macabre affrescate nelle chiese (. . .) Era una sensazione nuova e
> strana possedere uno scheletro, penetrando nel sesso morbido e
> vivo che sembrava esservi rimasto impigliato un po' come un caldo nido di uccello rimane impigliato tra i rami secchi e freddi di
> un albero invernale. (. . .) Era proprio uno scheletro; e come uno
> scheletro giaceva scompostamente, piena di angoli retti ed acuti,
> dando l'impressione che ad una scossa tutte le ossa grandi e piccole di cui era composta potessero staccarsi le une dalle altre e ricadere in disordine sulle coperte. (25-26)

And in the story, "Che me ne faccio del carnevale," the male protagonist observes, "E' la morte o meglio una donna che, chissà perché, si è mascherata da morte" (*La cosa* 193).

Again and again, even the female characters, as Moravia chooses to present them, consider the images appropriate to themselves. He never gives them the mental wherewithal to let them protest the metaphors and similes that render them either passive or decorative, either playthings or deathly images. In Moravia's world the women agree to them ("Va bene, sono la morte"); they even extend and embellish them. Being statues and madonnas, dolls and babies, objects, property to be bartered, and ultimately death itself, these highly image-ized women for the most part appear to sleepwalk through the novels where life acts upon them. They are rarely in control, either thematically or imagistically.

The categories of images – statues and madonnas, dolls and babies, objects of property, flowers and plants – have traditionally been associated with women in literature, but none-the-less they jar the reader's sensibilities within the cumulative context of Moravia's individual novels and short stories. If our response is one of outrage, it might be also conditioned and tempered by our expectations of (certainly not agreement with) this sort of description as business-as-usual. What we do not anticipate at first reading, however, is that there are not to be found in any convincing numbers the parallel categories conventionally associated with men (i.e., hunters, protectors, for example).

There *is*, however, one category predominantly reserved for men – that of abstract concepts. Similes and metaphors abound where the existence of a man (rarely of a woman) is equated with involved philosophical concepts or abstractions, i.e. the examples of a man being compared to an explosion in a China shop, and a wad of clothing tossed about in a washing machine. Also in *La noia*, the protagonist defines his existential desperation as the cross section of a jet engine: "Un po' come si può vedere, nelle vetrine delle compagnie aeree, lo spaccato di un motore di aeroplano, con tutti i suoi complicati e numerosi congegni. Era il meccanismo, appunto, della disperazione" (61).

These complicated images, at times requiring whole paragraphs to complete, connote an intricacy that by implication makes the man's nature of existence, his brain, or his *noia* just as complicated in the comparison. The economically and concretely worded images devoted to women do not suffice for men, who require more lengthy elaborations and more involved image-izations.[3]

Women rarely describe themselves nor are they often described by the narrators as being anything remotely connected to an abstract, intellectual, philosophical, existential, or even moderately complex concept. Women are not given the luxury of much signif-

---

[3] Perhaps these existential crises in the Moravian male harken back to and find their solution in the young Moravia of *Gli indifferenti* whose Michele longs for the days when "si versavano vere lacrime per vere sciagure, e tutti gli uomini erano fatti di carne ed ossa e attaccati alla realtà come alberi alla terra" (234).

icant imagery of human experience. Sharon Wood writes that "The Moravian existential spirit is specifically male, even in a novel such as *La romana*; it is Mino, not Adriana who plays out the existential drama of the novel. Adriana's only choice is a paradoxical one, whether or not to accept and acknowledge her essential nature which would destine her to be a whore" (4-5).

In Moravia's view, "La donna ama solo il potere, quello sociale, o la potenza fisica, che è quella che sappiamo. Perché la donna è incaricata alla natura di perpetuare la specie, quindi va dietro al potere, magari scegliendosi un uomo che le faccia fare un figlio bello, forte, sano" (Romani). This antediluvian view of womanhood confirms Cottrell's observation that "Apparently a Moravian female need only exude sensuality; she may be only semi-literate or even totally illiterate, but in no case does she have intellectual interests, nor is she portrayed as being a thinking being. She lives by animal-like instincts and for sensual pleasure.

Only Adriana (*La romana*) and Cesira (*La ciociara*) are deeply troubled by periods of philosophical crises (although short-lived ones that are quickly resolved). It is for the Moravian male to suffer at length, and to prolong his suffering through conscious intellectualization of his problems. Moravia's one-sided, mindless women characters are one of the least satisfying aspects of his writing" (10).

Cottrell points out further that "the woman always seems to remain intact while the man crumbles – for the Moravian intellectual is portrayed as being spiritually impotent" (12). Through imagery, a woman is presented as the sum of her body parts, devoid of any disintegratable mental apparatus. Moravia never speaks of a woman's soul; her body is the stand-in for her spirit, and even then only as she relates to men.

Most images devoted to women are solid ones (teacher, actress, baby, jewel); moreover, most of them carry negative connotations (a burnt-out candle, a devourer, a witch, a scarecrow). This is at times true of men, but is especially and overwhelmingly so of women. One glance at women who are body parts/flowers/plants, etc. points up this fact. In the floral world, women are depicted as dead or dried flowers, unwatered plants, unopened buds, squashed geraniums, undesirable grass, non-clinging vines, plants left to die, and upside-down roses: almost always aberrations of nature or distorted negations of what is pleasing from the natural world. (Compare these images with those of men who appear as robust trees, fresh flowers and even whole vineyards.)

An especially compelling aspect of Moravia's image choices is the kinship between his metaphors and similes for women as plants and how they relate to images of death, where women are death itself or otherwise likened to skeletons, mummies, angels of death, and decapitated beings.

In *Metaphor as Cool Reason*, Lakoff and Turner draw some interesting parallels between conventional metaphors of plant life and metaphors of death, and how these images govern our speech patterns and, indeed, our entire way of thinking in Western culture. The authors explore how "metaphor resides in thought, not just in words"; they use their "people as plants" and death imagery to explicate a number of poems in the English language. They show that without a thorough grounding in our common use of much conventional imagery, we cannot understand a great deal of our own literature.

"As Psalm 103 says, 'As for man, his days are as grass: as a flower of the field, so he flourisheth.' Death comes with the harvest and the falling of the leaves. The stages of the plants and parts of plants in their yearly cycle correspond to the stages of life. When we speak of someone as 'a young sprout,' we mean that he is in the early stages of life. Someone 'in full bloom' is mature. Someone 'withering away' is approaching death" (6). "A standard way of understanding and talking about the life cycle is in terms of a metaphor according to which people are plants or parts of plants and a human life corresponds to a plant's life cycle" (12).

Plant life and death are connected both metaphorically and literally, not only in our minds but as a fact of our ecology. Moravia invents women who are decaying and dying plants, and he also invents those who are death. On a grand level, the result is an entanglement of imagery that coalesces into a very disturbing idea. Women are decaying organic material; they are death. Men are vigorous plants; they are alive and engaged in the full act of being human.

Lakoff and Turner talk about the relatively few archetypal metaphors that have entered into our common Western languages – life as burden; death as sleep; life as a year; death as winter; life as a journey; death as the destination. What Moravia adds to that model is the splitting or separation of archetypal metaphor (people/plants) between the sexes. He ascribes to women the larger share of metaphors with negative implications.

Human fantasy is strong "empowering us to make and understand even bizarre connections (. . .) PEOPLE ARE PLANTS gives us a basis for personifying death as something associated with plants . . ." (Lakoff and Turner 26). So the dangers in presenting women as plants are that women then are also equated with the ensuing and inevitable destructiveness and finality of death. (Yet, even when Moravia presents a deathly, skeletal woman, her sex organ is metaphorized as a warm bird's nest in a dry, cold tree branch in winter (*L'attenzione* 25).)

There is a certain power inherent in these images which have an "ability to create structure in our understanding of life. (. . .) Much of our reasoning about life involves inferences. Thus, the power to reason about so abstract an idea as life comes very largely through metaphor" (Lakoff and Turner 62). Even if Moravia only presented women as plants (and never even mentioned women as death), the implication of death would be just as present because of the kinds and numbers of negative plant life used to describe women. But Moravia's end result is all the stronger because he *does,* in fact, add deathly images to the equation, perhaps not wanting to rely on the reader's innate understanding of archetypal concepts and how they work.

> We understand and reason using our conceptual system, which includes an inventory of structures of which schemas and metaphors are established parts. Once we learn a schema, we do not have to learn it again or make it up fresh each time we use it. It becomes conventionalized and as such is used automatically, effortlessly, and even unconsciously. That is part of the power of schemas: we can use these ready tools without having to put any energy into making or finding them. Similarly, once we learn a conceptual metaphor, it too is just there, conventionalized, a ready and powerful conceptual tool – automatic, effortless, and largely unconscious. The things most alive in our conceptual system are those things that we use constantly, unconsciously and automatically (62).

> For the same reasons that schemas and metaphors give us power to conceptualize and reason, so they have power over us. Anything that we rely on constantly, unconsciously, and automatically is so much part of us that it cannot be easily resisted, in large measure because it is barely even noticed. To the extent that we use a conceptual schema or a conceptual metaphor, we

accept its validity. Consequently, when someone else uses it, we are predisposed to accept its validity. For this reason, conventionalized schemas and metaphors have persuasive power over us. (Lakoff and Turner 63)

A woman often will appear as the surreal, fragmentable sum of her physical parts.[4] Her face is a half-empty bag, her mouth is a shapeless gash or a plunger. Her genitalia form a cigar snipper. Her breasts are so large she has to hold them up like a baby. Her abdomen is an old suitcase. Her legs are two clubs. Her thighs are the jaws of a clamp. Her skin is a sail without wind. Her body is a pillow tied in two, and these are only 10 of about 70 different, negative image-izations referring to women's body parts.[5]

Insulting as they may be to women, the images are exceptionally innovative. With imagery Moravia does not just point up similarities that we may already recognize. On the contrary, his images provide new ways of conceptualizing the familiar. That picture of a sail without wind is vivid and clear; the pillow tied in two needs no further elaboration or embellishment. Moravia flourishes his rich imagination in these bizarre images; like the Baroque poet, he amazes with his inventiveness.

The context in which certain images function, and the aims of each individual work vis-à-vis the number and kinds of images that appear in it, are illuminating. They allow us to see why that particular imagery is assigned to each character. That kind of critical activity is fruitful and essential. For example, the *Racconti romani* and the *Nuovi racconti romani* have slightly different aims than do the novels, among which to reproduce the highly imagistic *romanaccio* speech. Consequently many images in those works are as colorful and vivid as the Roman oral tradition itself. Yet, on another level all the images when collected and viewed apart from their specific, primary function within that given work, have a radically different effect. At times they offer a sort of collective image. This is sometimes

---

[4] For an interesting discussion of surrealism's influence upon Moravia, see Moravia and Elkann (242).

[5] See respectively *Io e lui* 254, 26, 25, 79; *Nuovi racconti romani*, "Non è il momento," 363 and "Rigoletta," 141; *L'attenzione* 178; *Boh!* 226; *La cosa* 16; *1934* 30. Jane Cottrell points out that "in Moravia's fictional world, physicality is so continually emphasized that if there is any other dimension it is imperceptible to his characters" (8).

produced, for example, by the veritable cascade of negativity relating to the female body, where a paradigm soon developes in the reader's mind as a set stereotype, and herein lies the danger of image-ization. [6] With the complicity of imagery, something very uncomplimentary to women happens in Moravia's prose; that "something" is both created and underlined by the abundant imagery which emphasizes his literal, negative physical descriptions.

Just one example of woman-as-animal suffices to highlight some of the ferocious negativity inherent in that particular category – a passage from the short story, "Un dritto": "(C)i aveva una testolina d'uccello, senza carne, col naso a becco e gli occhi spiritati, che quando parlava, uno gli veniva fatto di tirarsi indietro, come di fronte a un nibbio o a un falco inferocito. Aveva la voce aspra e brutta, la signora Lurini, proprio di cornacchia" (NRR 94-95). Not only are the women animals, but rapacious animals. [7] Positive ani-

---

[6] Cottrell finds that Moravia's females "tend to be of three distinct types: earth-mother figures who are well-proportioned but rather too ample and filled-out; those who have sensual but distorted bodies, with a head too large, legs too short and stocky, bust too pendulous and hips too narrow or too large; and occasionally, in the later works, small-breasted women who have become asexual through adoption of middle-class values, or who have abnormal sexual tastes" (8-9). In his review of La villa del venerdì, Renato Minore describes Moravia's typical woman as "quarantenne allo stesso tempo invitante e sfuggente, stretta al laccio di una carnalità che la guida e la prostra, la signora Burla è un altro personaggio estratto dall'universo moraviano. Pazza, ninfomane, moglie delusa: non c'è che l'imbarazzo della scelta." Predictably all the images used to describe these women are consonant with Cottrell's and Minore's types; the imagery underlines them and makes them more vividly stereotypical. Crocenzi and Fernandez also consider the physicality of Moravia's women. Crocenzi separates the corpulent Moravian women from the thin ones. "Le donne moraviane quando sono magre, sono generalmente di una magrezza eccessiva, incavata, consumata da ambigui ardori interiori che sembrano aver succhiato via la carne dal loro corpo. Sono rinsecchite, piuttosto che magre, arse da cupidi pensieri e brama di predominio. Spesso, è la smaniosa avidità di denaro, l'arcigna avarizia, la caparbia volontà di arrivare a mutar stato che le fa bruciare di fiamme insane: e perciò, tanto spesso, questi tipi di donne affollano gli ambienti borghesi o piccolo borghesi" (39). Crocenzi adds, "Se invece sono giovani e belle di corpo, hanno spesso o un viso insignificante o la traccia di una vaga rassomiglianza con un uccello o una scimmia" (34).

Dominique Fernandez separates the popolane from the borghesucce: "Le donne placide, opulenti, di carattere dolce, sono donne del popolo, mentre le creature sdegnose, distanti freddamente muscolose e lombate, fan parte della borghesia, e forse Moravia ha voluto indicare con questo dettaglio che le prime rispettano e seguono un ordine naturale, mentre le seconde portano fin nel loro corpo le stigmate di un'esistenza falsa" (56-57).

[7] Sharon Wood alludes to Pullini's notion that woman's animal appetites threaten the sanctity of marriage. L'amore coniugale, for example, is about wicked wives who have a "fiery animal nature" (3).

mal associations are reserved for men. Paul Ricoeur has written, "il faut toujours deux idées pour faire une métaphore" (31); "bien métaphoriser c'est apercevoir le semblable" (34). ("It takes *two* ideas to make a metaphor" (21, italics mine).) When Moravia metaphorizes he creates resemblances where before there were none in the reader's perception, and the *semblances* between women and animals are disturbing.

Moravia's uncomplimentary physical descriptions of women echo one of his major themes: that neither the spiritual/existential *modus vivendi* (the approach favored mostly by male characters), nor dwelling on the physical aspects of life (as lived mostly by female characters), suffices as a code for facing the magnitude of our own existence. So that when a woman's body falls apart, decays or goes from fat to thin or vice versa in a Moravian work, men are simply reminded that not even the promise of good sex with an attractive partner can attenuate the effects of his alienation (and in "L'uomo come fine" Moravia defines alienation as something quite contrary to completeness and lastingness).[8]

As an arranged collection of images cutting across all of his works, in their accumulation simile and metaphor seem to carry on of their own accord. Whether intended to do so by the author or not, this use of imagery reminds one in many ways of the now-prohibited "subliminal messages" which in the 1950's used to be projected rapidly and surreptitiously during commercial films urging the viewer's subconscious to "eat popcorn" or "get a beverage." Recent articles by Goldman, Miller and Crispin examine recurring interest in such mental manipulations. Despite some reservations, it is still widely thought that these messages have serious effects. Colin Murray Turbayne points out that "A story often told – like advertising and propaganda – comes to be believed more seriously. Those

---

    [8] Crocenzi observes: "Tutto in Moravia si decompone; non reggono i sentimenti che marciscono sotto il grondare dei soliloqui degli esasperanti interrogatori con se stessi che sono generati da cervelli disperatamente spogli di altri interessi e da anime sbattute e svuotate dalla inesorabilità della condizione umana; non reggono appigli materiali di altra natura che potrebbero stabilire un insieme di rapporti con il prossimo e con gli oggetti, perché il denaro, ad esempio, non salva l'uomo ma lo limita, lo chiude lo soffoca" (37); "quando il corpo della donna, comincia a morire, non c'è più scampo neanche per l'unica porta di salvezza perché non è più possibile l'unico rapporto con il mondo. E la donna giacerà come oggetto inutile e l'uomo perirà incatenato ai suoi stessi problemi che non troveranno più il grembo in cui annullarsi" (38).

details stressed tend to stay stressed while those suppressed tend to stay suppressed until another effective metaphor restores them" (21).

After reading well over 400 times that women *are* one animal or another in just 15 different works (see table below), the cumulative effect is impressive. When we read over 90 different instances in which women's body parts are likened to the most improbable assortment of gadgets and wacky objects (cigar snippers, wet coal, bars of soap, yellowed, old bed sheets) in fewer than 10 works, we become desensitized to these dehumanizing fragmentations of the whole being. What are we to make of this barrage of images where the female body is emasculating (cigar snippers!), enticing yet perilous, pampering but vicious, and most often belittled, ridiculed and humiliated?

The category of women-as-animals includes the rapacious (birds, lions, wolves, crabs), the passive (sheep, cows), the parasitic (leeches), the sacrificial (goats, lambs), the poisonous (insects, spiders), the big and obtuse (dinosaurs, elephants, whales, donkeys, bears), the weak (rabbits), the strong (horses), the faithful (dogs), the aggressive (roosters), the sneaky and slippery (cats, snakes, foxes, seals), the graceful (swans, deer, butterflies), the pesky and annoying (chickens, mice), the animals for slaughter (cattle, butchermeat), the fierce (caged beasts of various kinds), the two-faced and deceitful (chameleons), the silly and insignificant (monkeys, geese), the disgusting and filthy (pigs, sows), the insensitive (rhinoceros).

An imagistic suffocation ensues when one negative image is piled upon another in an overwhelming accumulation. As Christine Brooke-Rose has observed, "Metaphor is not merely the perception of similarity in dissimilarity, it is the changing of words by one another" (93). Woman becomes the object to which she is compared; what she is likened to takes on her characteristics. The differentiation eventually becomes hazy. Peter McGrath in an article entitled, "The Lessons of Munich," says that "Metaphors tend to obscure the differences between things or situations. Moreover, their power is essentially nonrational. They make a direct appeal to the emotions. That is the whole point of using them. The purpose of metaphors is not so much to instruct as to arouse . . . As the novelist Walker Percy once pointed out, metaphor is always "wrong," literally speaking; it says that one thing is another, as in the suggestion that love is a rose or war is hell. Worse, he adds, it is likely to be most persuasive precisely when it is most wrong" (37).

These quasi-subliminal image-messages become a literary short-hand in Moravia's writing. Over 50 times in the same five or six novels, women are presented as consumable items. One could construct an entire, multi-course, sumptuous Italian meal from the gamut of edibles used to describe women: vegetables from Savoy cabbage to onions to pumpkins; meat, steak, chicken, eggs, omelets, breads, chestnuts, *pasta sfusa,* various basic ingredients from flour to sugar. She becomes an Arcimboldo painting of every fruit imaginable, and she is equated finally both with the liqueurs and the dessert. This abundant food imagery cannot be dismissed simply as the stereotypical "Italian" preoccupation with eating well, because food analogies not connected to individual characters appear in only three other instances. Further, men are represented by food imagery only twelve times and never negatively.[9]

Lakoff and Turner write convincingly on the power unleashed by a plenitude of imagery. "The coherence among metaphors is a major source of the power of poetry. By forming a comparison of several basic metaphors, a poet draws upon the grounding of those metaphors in common experience and knowledge. When that experience and knowledge cohere, the metaphors seem all the more natural and compelling. Complex metaphors grip us partly because they awake in us the experience and knowledge that form the grounding of those metaphors, partly because they make the coherence of that experience and knowledge resonate, and partly because they lead us to form new coherences in what we know and experience" (89). We are indebted to the study of semiotics which allows us to understand fully that the sign often gets taken for the signified, as the ensemble of Moravia's cornucopia of food imagery conflates with the stereotypical idea that women are for consumption no more or less than a steaming plate of *fettuccine.*

Women are statues, sphynxes, decorative monsters more than 60 times; women are marionettes, dolls, and puppets more than 40

---

[9] In an interesting admixture of metaphor and simile in *Gli indifferenti,* Leo is near exhaustion from Carla's insatiable sexual appetite. Leo compares his (in)ability to satisfy Carla to a banquet where women are not only equated directly with the wine and food, but they become beasts at the same time. "Era un sentimento sgradevole e preciso d'incapacità, come dire? d'impotenza: era come se per saziarlo, gli avessero offerto dei barilli traboccanti di vino, delle immense tavole piegate sotto il peso d'ogni più prelibata vivanda e degli appartamenti rigurgitanti delle più belle donne del mondo distese e ammucchiate le une sulle altre come tante bestie" (259).

times; women are objects of property and commercial products more than 30 times; women are masks, machines, flowers and plants (mostly in their negativity); and most startlingly they are "death" more than 20 times. But, with the possible exception of Carla (*Gli indifferenti*), Adriana (*La romana*), and Cesira (*La ciociara*), they are rarely living, breathing, thinking, anguishing and existing women. As Minore describes the typical Moravian woman, she is a "vero e proprio automa che muove i comportamenti degli altri senza alcuna coscienza (se non minima, baluginante) di se stessa." Significantly in the case of the above three who do have a rudimentary existential life, the first two effectively become prostitutes; so does the daughter of the third.

In a compelling article in the *New York Review,* Denis Donoghue paraphrases Paul de Man's questions about metaphor. " . . . de Man directs his suspicion against metaphor and indeed against any claim to knowledge. In *Allegories of Reading* he says, correctly, that metaphor is 'an exchange or substitution of properties on the basis of resemblance'; a process made possible 'by a proximity or an analogy so close and intimate that it allows the one to substitute for the other without revealing the difference necessarily introduced by the substitution.' Other theorists have emphasized rather the tension between resemblance and difference in metaphor, and have thought metaphors good precisely to the degree to which the tension is maintained. (. . .) But de Man suggested that in metaphor the mind wants to suppress differences and to enforce resemblance to the point of what he called 'totalization' – total identity" (32-37). If de Man is correct, and if differences between tenor and vehicle are indeed suppressed, then the final aggregate image of woman in Moravia's works is all the more potent in a negative sense; it becomes redoubled, first "literally" then figuratively.

Cottrell concludes that Moravia simply "does not understand women very well. His ideas about female sexuality appear ill-informed, or at best, not representative of the great majority of women." In many of his depictions she finds him "self-indulgent and wish-fulfilling" (11). Crocenzi is less charitable. "Il rapporto infatti che lega Moravia alla donna è un rapporto di ostilità: tanto acre in lui si avverte il gusto, la voluttà, diremmo, di denigrarla, offenderla, immiserirla, anche quando, come accade in alcuni personaggi dei suoi romanzi e racconti di più felice esito artistico o, comunque, di maggior risonanza, sembra, a prima vista, disposto ad un più cordiale incontro con le sue creature femminili, o intento, addirittura, a sollevarle in una luce di simpatia" (5).

To add Turbayne's voice to the Italian feminist perspective, he too cautions against the negative effect of collective-imagistic presentations, the kinds that are found in these works: "The human characteristics that Aesop pretended were owned by animals have become literally part of their equipment. We no longer make believe that foxes are cunning and lambs gentle. They are. (. . .) There is a difference between using a metaphor and being used by it, between using a model and mistaking the model for the thing modeled. The one is to make believe that something is the case; the other is to believe it" (22). Time and again in the same few novels and short stories, women are "something else." Willy-nilly Moravia eventually has us "mistaking the model for the modeled." After reading literally hundreds of his images, inevitably any casual reader will become innured to the many instances of ostensibly harmless word play which, however, rarely concede to women the same complex problems that men have, and which cast her in every possible light, save a positive one. [10]

Foster Tait considers the disadvantages of taking literally an image that may become a model. "For example, to take as literally true one of the numerous models which occur in science would be to attribute the model to the world. It would be to say, in effect, that the world 'really is that way.' But this is not a useful way to approach either the world, knowledge, or science. It is not because it minimizes the possibility of employing other models to illustrate the facts in question" (27). Similarly Moravia's constantly calling a woman a tomato or a slimy animal or consistently referring to her as a piece of fruit to be picked and eaten implies that she "really is

---

[10] Despite the sometimes strident tone of their work, Liliana Caruso and Bibi Tomasi do make some valid observations about Moravia in *I padri della fallocultura*: "Indifferenza, ambizione, noia tormentano l'animo dei personaggi maschili; quelli femminili, anche se travolti dalle medesime situazioni, sono volti più al fare che al pensare, più al subire che al reagire" (11). Cottrell agrees: "All in all, the male characters have been more satisfactory creations than the females. In fact, almost all Moravia's women have been depressingly shallow and unbelievable creatures. Perhaps Colette put her finger on part of the problem when she asked herself, "Why is it that a man can never talk about a woman's sexual nature without making incredibly stupid remarks?" (140). And Crocenzi bluntly concludes: "Moravia: autore diseducativo per la formazione di una coscienza femminile; disgregatore della donna già in atto, amaro e senza speranza per la donna del futuro" (107).

that way," precluding any attribution of an intellectual life to that woman or any kind of normal rapport with men that would put her on an equal basis. The male-female rapport lacks any reciprocal meeting of the minds or authentic exchange of ideas. The woman is functional, but she is no more than that.

Moravia himself fans the fire of this issue in an interview with Cinzia Romani where he observes, "Il protagonista è sempre l'uomo, in quanto è lui a fornire il giudizio morale sulle cose. (. . .) E' l'uomo, invece, che idealizza la donna, perché la ritiene simbolo della cultura. (. . .) Per me le donne hanno un'anima e mezza, è solo che le donne hanno bisogno di assicurarsi un destino, per sè, per i propri figli, quindi il loro tempo per la conoscenza è limitato. Loro sono molto più forti dell'uomo, ma nei miei racconti è sempre l'uomo l'essere morale, colui che fornisce un giudizio etico." [11] Women are distanced and held at arm's length in great part through the use of imagery. Max Black points out that metaphor is a "screen" which "filters" the facts of the world for us, elucidating some aspects more than others. It causes "shifts in meaning" (292). In Moravia's writing our perception of women's existence is indeed "filtered." We see everything refracted through metaphor and simile. "Suppose I look at the night sky through a piece of heavily smoked glass on which certain lines have been left clear. Then I shall see only the stars that can be made to lie on the lines previously prepared upon the screen, and the stars I do see will be seen as organised by the screen's structure. We can think of metaphor as such a screen . . ." (Black 288).

Through this screen women become something "Other," and as such, the male protagonists are excused from having to deal with them as individuals, and are free to go about contemplating their angst, oblivious to the notion that until they come to human terms with the other half of the population, they will not solve their own problems of existence.

---

[11] Caruso and Tomasi expound at great length about the objectivization of women in Moravia's prose. Referring to Tarcisio in the short story, "Il ritorno dalla villeggiatura," from the collection, *L'amante infelice*, they note: "(S)i lamenta della propria esistenza, è tormentato dalla noia, è alla ricerca di qualche cosa che lo tragga fuori dal torpore; ovviamente pensa alle donne in quanto esse possono essere delle occasioni propizie per fargli dimenticare il tedio della propria esistenza: le donne e il loro possesso sono utili ai maschi, sostenendoli nei loro vaneggiamenti esistenziali, unicamente come oggetti di godimento sessuale, non certo come persone con cui avere un rapporto alla pari" (7-8).

Terry Eagleton's paraphrase of Julia Kristeva accurately represents the effect of Moravia's novels: "Women are represented within male-governed society, fixed by sign, image, meaning, yet because they are also the 'negative' of that social order there is always in them something which is left over, superfluous, unrepresentable, which refuses to be figured there" (190). Moravia fixes women through imagery, robbing them of wholeness; but the reader senses that something is missing.

Throughout *Models and Metaphors* Max Black makes clear that each metaphor has two facets, the main one and the collateral one. Both carry their own cognitive baggage, as they parallel each other in meaning. In thinking about both sets of notions, the reader perceives a kind of cross-over in meaning both from A to B and back from B to A. The two concepts begin to blur until the end result is one thought not two. This phenomenon can be a treacherous one, indeed, when the imagery is always negative. The tenor becomes the vehicle; certain connotations are forced onto the female characters.

The danger of such image-izing is embodied most clearly in the image where the woman is likened to a sea cucumber, a tube shaped, marine animal that has a mouth at one end and an anus at the other. In *La vita interiore* Desideria describes herself the way she used to be before she (thinks) she reached a "higher consciousness":

> un pezzo di carne inanimata e smaniosa, un buco circondato da un corpo, un'oloturia. (. . .) L'oloturia è un organismo marino intermedio tra gli animali e le piante, dal corpo allungato, in cui si distingue un'estremità anteriore in cui si apre la bocca, una posteriore in cui si apre l'ano. Insomma, una specie di cetriolo. Cioè un essere di forma cilindrica, compatto, massiccio, sordo, ottuso, cieco, un vero e proprio tubo digerente rivestito di carne, dotato di una vitalità, appunto smaniosa, fatta di contrazioni e di spasmi puramente fisici. Quest'essere, questa oloturia sarei stata io (51).

A constant link is made between women and uselessness, dumbness, and purely functional, utilitarian sexuality, the sea-cucumber imagery being one of the most flagrant examples. Put less politely, for Caruso and Tomasi women in Moravia's prose are "solo inettitudine e vagina" (14). At the same time, the female genitals are image-ized over and over again until they become detached and separated from any human values; they are linked both to pure sexual gratification and to the scary aspects of castration (thighs as clamp, genitals as cigar snippers). Thus, it becomes far easier for the protagonists (and, in unfortunate cases, the reader) simply to consider a woman's genitals *pars pro toto* and not even bother to deal with the other end.

The protagonist of *La noia*'s dismissal of the whole woman is typical: ". . . io non potevo fare a meno di confrontare la fenditura orizzontale della bocca con quella verticale del sesso e di notare, meravigliato, quanto la seconda fosse più espressiva della prima, appunto nella maniera tutta psicologica che è propria a quei tratti del viso nei quali si rivela il carattere della persona" (174). Moravia first creates the similarities through metaphor and simile, and then he treats the metaphoric referents, the vehicles, as though *they* were the reality. Moravia is very clever at making metaphoric link-ups, at connecting two spheres of knowledge; as Black states: "It would be more illuminating in some of these cases to say that the metaphor creates the similarity than to say that it formulates some similarity antecedently existing" (Black 284-85). Indeed, those similarities did not exist before Moravia purposefully invented them.

Moravia's attention to women's problems has been noticed by critics in so far as women do appear as protagonists in two of his better works, *La ciociara* and *La romana*, but in the former Cesira's life is defined in terms of her day-to-day life and survival, and in the latter, Adriana's existence is couched in her affective sexual relations with men. Neither is overly concerned with what is going on in her own head or with the nature of her own existence. With few exceptions throughout his complete works, women figure prominently only as foil to the problems of the twentieth-century man who, on the contrary, is *deeply* concerned with what transpires in his mind.

Women are often juxtaposed imagistically with parallel images related to men. For example, in *La ciociara* women-as-animals for slaughter are linked to men-as-butchers; women-as-sacrificial-lambs are posed against men-as-high-priest. In *Io e lui* a man clings to a woman like a drowning man to the mast of a sinking ship. [12] In

---

[12] Alberto Moravia, *Io e lui*, "A questo pensiero mi stringo con più forza alle gambe di Irene che le mie braccia circondano disperatamente, come le braccia del naufrago circondano l'albero disarmato della nave che affonda . . ." (92).

"L'odore nel naso" the man is a "poetic appendix" to the woman's vulgar personality.[13] Women are adjunct to men, as Sharon Wood states: "Female gender in the novels of Moravia operates on a level of difference by and against which the central, substantive male presence can establish itself" (19).

The dovetailing of the metaphors and similes, as we have seen, forms a complicated mesh where the splicing and blurring of the male and female characters' images are related solely to the fleshing-out of the male protagonist. In most instances of parallel imagery, the female metaphor is created for the fuller character development of the male protagonist, and rarely vice versa. For example, the antinomy of "poetic appendix/vulgar personality" exists to complete Moravia's more careful description of the male protagonist. It adds little to our understanding of the woman, but might elucidate what we can know about men in general (and Moravia in particular), if one considers the Derridean model as discussed by Terry Eagleton:

> Woman is the opposite, the 'other' of man: she is non-man, defective man, assigned a chiefly negative value in relation to the male first principle. But equally man is what he is only by virtue of ceaselessly shutting out this other or opposite, defining himself in antithesis to it, and his whole identity is therefore caught up and put at risk in the very gesture by which he seeks to assert his unique, autonomous existence. Woman is not just an other in the sense of something beyond his ken, but an other intimately related to him as the image of what he is not, and therefore as an essential reminder of what he is. Man therefore needs this other even as he spurns it, is constrained to give a positive identity to what he regards as no-thing. Not only is his own being parasitically dependent upon the woman, and upon the act of excluding and subordinating her, but one reason why such exclusion is necessary is because she may not be quite so other after all. Perhaps she stands as a sign of something in man himself which he needs to repress, expel beyond his own being, relegate to a securely alien region beyond his own definitive limits. Perhaps what is outside is also somehow inside, what is alien also intimate – so that man needs to police the absolute frontier be-

---

[13] Alberto Moravia, *Boh!*, ". . . facendomi diventare l'appendice poetica della sua volgarissima personalità" (83).

tween the two realms as vigilantly as he does just because it may always be transgressed, has always been transgressed already, and is much less absolute than it appears. (132-33)

Are women so fearsome that they must be banished to this "alien region" beyond the Moravian male limits? Is that what all the distancing and fragmentation are about? Men are image-ized in Moravia's works over 600 times, but the overall effect is diluted (a) by the much greater number of comparable female-oriented images (about 850), (b) by scattering the images over a wider range of novels thus diluting the effect, and (c) by attributing to men a large category of sympathetic, intellectually abstract images. Over 75 times men are complex concepts, or they think existentially image-ized thoughts, or they have existential medical/mental problems described with similes and metaphors, or they suffer from *noia* in a metaphorical way. Men have more complete, well-rounded lives. Men think, suffer and exist; they have cornered the market on profound thought. [14]

There are approximately 100 fewer male-related animal images than female-related ones. As these are found in relatively few novels, they are less concentrated. There is not that same intensity of bombardment as there is in the constantly reappearing images of women as animals. In addition, the vehicle-animals used to describe males are not presented quite as negatively as they are for women. While the percentage of men-as-animals in relation to men-as-everything else is greater than that for women-as-animals in relation to women-as-everything else, all in all, much of the male-related animal imagery is more warm and friendly (". . . buono buono . . . un agnello" (*RR,* "I gioielli" 131)). The positive connotations of being *buono, buono* like an *agnello* rarely if ever appear to describe women.

Interesting as well is that in the category of food imagery, men are connected with food only 12 times (as compared to over 55 times for women); with body parts about 75 times (as compared to

---

[14] In his essay, "L'uomo e il personaggio," Moravia talks precisely about man's alienation: "L'uomo moderno non sarebbe che un'entità numerica dentro collettività tra le più formidabili che l'umanità abbia mai conosciuto. Esso non esisterebbe per sè solo ma come parte di qualcos'altro, di un organismo, di un sentimento, di un concetto collettivo. Con un tale uomo è ben difficile fare un personaggio, almeno nel senso tradizionale della parola" (*L'uomo come fine* 19).

over 100 times for women); with marionettes and puppets about
15 times (as compared to about 40 times for women); with machines and automata 7 times (as compared to about 20 times for
women).[15]
If one could ignore the numerous instances of undeniable sex-
ism in Moravia's writing ("Amicizia è bella finchè non c'è la donna"
(*RR* 109)), one might consider perhaps that he is making an important statement about contemporary attitudes which are not necessarily his own. Could it be that Moravia redeems his alleged misog-
yny by depicting women as he does to protest sincerely and to
correct that very phenomenon? Moravia does have many women
deliberately and sometimes ironically represent themselves as de-
scriminated-against social tragedies – women who are fully aware of
their status, and who even refer to themselves in sarcastic, metaphoric terms. ("La bambola sono io" (*Boh!* 108); "La vitella non
sa scrivere; io sì" (*L'attenzione* 25).) Yet, in response to a question
put to him about his treatment of women, Moravia could have re-
deemed himself. Instead he responded:

> Mi sono limitato a esprimere molte volte il mio interesse per le
> donne, e ne ho spiegato le ragioni. Sono molto semplici: per un
> romanziere, la donna è interessante in quanto selvaggia, o al-
> meno per metà selvaggia, cioè non totalmente integrata nella so-
> cietà. Lasciamo stare le ragioni storiche che hanno prodotto
> questo suo mezzo *apartheid:* sono d'altronde piuttosto evidenti.
> Questo carattere semi-indomito, semi-selvaggio rende la donna,
> già di per sé, un personaggio drammatico. (*Intervista* 189)

Moravia sees women as not being fully integrated into society;
he situates them in the realm of the uncivilized. Woman is a man's
Other; woman is nature while man is civilization.[16] He looks at

---

[15] Taking stock of Moravia's male protagonists in general, Caruso and Tomasi
remark: "Questi personaggi compiono delle azioni: amano, ingannano, lavorano,
uccidono, torturano, cospirano, muovono, insomma l'ingranaggio sociale; le donne,
invece, subiscono, sono vittime di questo ingranaggio, non fanno e non possono far
nulla nè per muoverlo nè per modificarlo" (5). Along these same lines Donald
Heiney writes of the typical female character that, "she is in possession of the ele-
mental forces without being obliged to intellectualize them or even being aware of
them; it is the male who intellectualizes while the force itself slips from his grasp"
(19).

[16] As quoted by Wood, Pullini observes: "Woman is nature in whom man pen-
etrates and loses himself as if through a need to enter the material womb; but she

women as though he were examining a specimen under a microscope, as an interesting literary subject. If he does consider women's social state a kind of shameful *apartheid,* one would expect him to express some outrage. Yet he does not. Instead, bizarre, negative images abound in his composite depiction of women as seen through the eyes of his alienated protagonist-narrators. Women are never focalizers; all information about them is channelled through men. He never redeems himself, neither literarily nor publicly nor in the press.

Conceivably he could be likened to a Machiavelli, in that he is not writing about what *should* be, but about what *is.* One could be unjaundiced and entertain the notion that perhaps he is not telling us what he thinks of women, but what his *narrators* think of them – narrators who, for the most part, are both among the most maladjusted in twentieth-century prose, and at the same time, most representative of these post-war decades. Indeed in Moravia's own words, fictional characters "dicono spesso il contrario di quello che avrebbe voluto far dire loro l'autore" (*L'uomo come fine* 219).

In the article, "Differenza tra artista e intellettuale" in *Il Corriere della Sera,* Moravia makes it clear that it is the artist's task to mirror reality, and Cottrell points out that for Moravia fiction is "an incarnation of a subjective reality; furthermore its aim is didactic" (19). Yet, no reasonable reader can ignore or fail to be dismayed by the overwhelming and unredeemed negative light cast upon women in his novels. He never even hints that his writing is corrective or parodistic.

Detailed study of all of Moravia's works shows that while image-ization in some way is diachronic in his writing, the greatest number of images is concentrated in a few works. Those works are listed below with in parentheses their dates of publication and the average number of similes and/or metaphors per page, in descending order of image-frequency. While the rubric, "images per page," smacks of pseudo-science, and clearly can never be adopted as an invariable, it is nevertheless useful to see which of Moravia's periods reveal the densest imagery. To be sure, by presenting the following table, it is acknowledged that the "page" can never be an

---

can become damnation when she does not return the male love or when she herself loses control of her instinctivity and burns, in unfitting times and ways, with insatiable appetites" (3).

invariable; and, no scientific or methodological implication is made of anything beyond the obvious: that some works feature more images than others, and that those works seem to cluster in his later, post-war writing.

1. *La ciociara* (1965) 1 image every 2.45 pages
2. *Racconti romani* (1954) 1 image every 2.5 pages [17]
3. *Nuovi racconti romani* (1959) 1 image every 2.7 pages
4. *Il paradiso* (1970) 1 image every 3.6 pages
5. *Io e lui* (1971) 1 image every 3.8 pages
6. *La noia* (1960) 1 image every 3.8 pages
7. *La cosa* (1983) 1 image every 4.3 pages
8. *L'uomo che guarda* (1985) 1 image every 4.4 pages
9. *Boh!* (1976) 1 image every 4.6 pages
10. *1934* (1982) 1 image every 5.1 pages
11. *Un'altra vita* (1973) 1 image every 5.2 pages
12. *L'automa* (1962) 1 image every 5.9 pages
13. *La vita interiore* (1978) 1 image every 7 pages
14. *L'attenzione* (1965) 1 image every 7 pages
15. *Il conformista* (1951) 1 image every 7.7 pages

The most concerted use of imagery occurs after W.W. II, and continues into the last three decades, precisely from the 1960s to his last work, the period when with most intensity Moravia explores the fragmentation, dehumanization, and alienation of humanity. Compared with the density of images in these novels of the 1960s through the 1980s, the novel with the next greatest metaphor/page ratio is *La romana* (1947) with only 1 metaphor or simile about every 15 pages. The period after *La romana* is generally considered to usher in the beginnings of Moravia's more existential period. (In fact, Cottrell pinpoints that moment in *La romana* "where Adriana's first existential cries are described. At moments when she is alone,

---

[17] These two collections of short stories (*Racconti romani* and *Nuovi racconti romani*) are fraught with metaphors and similes. Perhaps the reason for this phenomenon lies in the fact that one of Moravia's aims in these stories, which were originally a series of newspaper short stories, was to try to reproduce the metaphorical Roman speech patterns. At a certain point in 1959, he discontinued writing them for the *Corriere della Sera,* saying they had become "di stesura troppo facile e scontata" (del Buono 62). Had he continued, one can only guess at the levels of imagistic density which would have resulted.

she suddenly becomes aware of the absurdity of human life and sees herself suspended in nothingness. After reaching a point of desperation, she drifts into a nonthinking state and eventually finds that she is the same Adriana as before" (69).)

It bears repeating that the categories of images are not simply random or infrequent, appearing once or twice here and there in Moravia's complete works; they are common occurrences which convincingly inform Moravia's prose narrative over the 60 years of his career. By tracing the images group by group, as they weave a pattern in and out of his works, it is evident that a superstructure imposes itself upon the complete works. Surely Moravia, himself, would have denied as a virtual impossibility his own *deliberate* orchestration of these images over the years, but as Umberto Eco points out, "When the writer says he has worked without giving any thought to the rules of the process, he simply means he was working without realizing he knew the rules" (11).

Barthes gives much importance to the allusiveness of style as it "plunges into the closed recollection of the person and achieves its opacity from a certain experience of matter; style is never anything but metaphor, that is, equivalence of the author's literary intention and carnal structure. (. . .) Style is always a secret; but the occult aspect of its implications does not arise from the mobile and ever provisional nature of language; its secret is recollection locked within the body of the writer. The allusive virtue of style is not a matter of speed, as in speech, where what is unsaid nevertheless remains as an interim of language, but a matter of density, for what stands firmly and deeply beneath style, brought together harshly or tenderly in its figures of speech, are fragments of a reality entirely alien to language" (*Writing* 12).[18]

Moravia's novels and short stories reside under a wide umbrella of simile and metaphor. He imbeds his descriptive imagery so neat-

---

[18] Along the same lines, Terry Eagleton writing about phenomenological criticism talks about the text being a reflection of the author's consciousness. "All of its stylistic and semantic aspects are grasped as organic parts of a complex totality, of which the unifying essence is the author's mind. To know this mind, we must not refer to anything we actually know of the author (. . .), but only to those aspects of his or her consciousness which manifest themselves in the work itself. Moreover, we are concerned with the 'deep structures' of this mind, which can be found in recurrent themes and patterns of imagery; and in grasping these we are grasping the way the writer 'lived' his world, the phenomenological relations between himself as subject and the world as object" (59).

ly within the storyline that the reader is hardly aware of its intensity and pervasiveness. Yet, this narrative architecture functions as one of the stylistic principles of a whole career of writing, and most concertedly in the later, post-war works, where imagery has a multi-leveled integration into the story-lines, and in many cases boasts a developmental progress unto itself.

The implications of what has been examined here are serious; for, over the span of his career, imagistically, Moravia has presented a life's work of women who are, for the most part, unthinking objects for consumption, play, barter, sale, dissection – almost everything, except for being equal partners in the existential journey of the male protagonist's functioning mind. While he also depicts men who are inept, at least they try to think their way out of their *abulia*.

With a clear picture of his construction of imagery and the subtext that it creates comes a fuller understanding of his major concerns, and of what perhaps unwittingly Moravia is telling us about himself, his characters and ourselves. It is the reader's task to try to sort out what it all means, to unravel the riddle. For imagery has a life of its own and invades Moravia's works with a seeming informality that eludes our attention at first reading. Only close scrutiny of his writing makes us aware of this pivotal, governing principle of style.

I V

SIMPLE ORCHESTRATION OF IMAGERY

> Scusami sono costretto ancora una volta a servirmi
> della metafora, ma è indispensabile.
>
> (Moravia, *Il viaggio a Roma* 49)

Recapitulating: at the simplest level, some of Moravia's images
are truly random. They serve the clear purpose of enriching the
prose; they help the reader see something in a way in which it has
not been seen before, to make connections that ordinarily one
would not think of making, and generally to fill semantic lacunae.
Taking a more complicated, subtextual view, Moravia's images can
be patterned, re-arranged, and examined apart from their immediate, basic function of simple, colorful description, or what Ricoeur
calls the "morceau brillant." When considered in this reorganized
way, the images operate on layered planes signifying more than
what is immediately evident, offering the possibility of multiple interpretations.[1] As such, they take on a whole new meaning; they
form a fascinating umbrella which governs especially most of Moravia's post-war work, but also cuts across his entire *opera omnia.*

Yet another function of imagery in Moravia's works is to operate entirely within the boundaries of a single prose piece, where imagery is orchestrated internally, and becomes an associate in the
narrative task of plot development. Moravia uses this technique of
orchestration to varying degrees in his works. A most elementary
example appears in *La ciociara* where the Fascist soldiers are devils
and the Allies are likened to the local patron saints who intercede

---

[1] See Lacan. *Ecrits/A Selection* 55.

alternately for rain and good weather. The imagistic interdependence of these groups parallels a much more complicated entanglement of metaphor and simile which describes the two protagonists, Cesira and Rosetta, of the same novel. Other examples are increasingly more complex.

In "Un dritto" Moravia tells us that if a one-kilo loaf of bread could have an expression of sadness, that would be the face of the protagonist's wife. ". . . e se una pagnotta di un chilo potesse avere una espressione di tristezza, ebbene avrebbe quella che subito notai sul viso ottuso e massiccio di Agnese" (*NRR* 93-97). Once it is established that the wife is a loaf of bread, the narrator then declares of the husband's philandering: "La pagnotta casareccia non gli piace più" (*NRR* 99).

Moravia uses a food image to describe the wife, and then continues that controlling metaphor as the key to the story – the husband no longer likes homemade bread. Metaphor works on two levels in this story: first, to describe the wife's face as something ordinary and boring, a "food" that her husband can have any day of the week; and second, to provide a basis for the eventual outcome of the story, simple as it may be.

As we have seen, women have often been depicted in "random" ways as food in Moravia's prose. In this instance embedding a narratively "functional" food image into the story is only new to the extent that its meaning is multi-layered: first, the bread image is an integral part of the story; and second, it underscores the fact that almost all of his other female characters are likened to food as well, albeit not necessarily in an orchestrated way.

In "Ritorno dal mare" (*I racconti di Moravia,* 1952), Lorenzo describes his wife: "Ella aveva un po' di scimmia, pensò Lorenzo: non tanto nei tratti quanto nell'espressione triste, decrepita e innocente, come è appunto quella di certe piccole bertucce. E come una scimmia, infatti, simulava un atteggiamento di dignità offesa di cui egli la sapeva del tutto incapace" (601-02).

Later he calls her a *puledro* and even sees her hair as a mane, "i capelli sconvolti dal vento" (603). Finally the metaphoric "set up" comes to fruition. He grabs her, shakes her, and shouts, " 'Rispondi, bestia . . . perché non rispondi?' " (610). As above, the images serve two purposes: a modest one which communicates on a simple, descriptive level, and another one which defines the woman as animal (a technique by now familiar to the reader).

Like the bread-faced wife whose husband no longer likes homemade bread, the *scimmia/bertuccia/puledro* becomes, in her husband's perception of reality, a *bestia* to be mistreated as Lorenzo might in his view rightfully abuse any of the animals to which he has likened her. Imagery in these two instances helps the husbands rationalize the demeaning way in which they treat their wives. It distances the wives; it depersonalizes them, allowing the husbands to dismiss their wives as they would a crust of bread or a beast of burden.

An equally interesting example appears in *L'attenzione.* "Il giornalaio è un uomo di quarant'anni, ossia, come si dice, nel fiore dell'età, con una faccia nera e rincagnata, piccoli occhi strabuzzati, naso adunco, mento che risale al naso, baffi ispidi fra naso e mento. Una faccia che offre una notevole somiglianza con quella di un cane da guardia stupido e feroce; e infatti, proprio come un cane da guardia nel proprio canile, se ne sta rintanato nell'edicola, pronto, si direbbe, ad azzannare la mano che si arrischia dentro per scegliere un giornale" (112).

First the newsman is a man; then a dog-like adjective for his face is added to the picture; next he resembles a dumb but fierce watchdog; then he is like a watchdog in his doghouse; and finally he is the dog which bites the hand of the buyer. The piling-on of canine image after image makes it possible for the initial dog-like qualities to evolve logically into a whole *quadro d'insieme* of dog life, dog actions, and the like. The example shows that men are not immune as targets of Moravia's animal imagery, and that Moravia can be playful with his prose style. His waggishness resides just on the surface of the narration, and it is not difficult within the flow of his prose to detect when he pauses simply to have fun with his mimetic fantasy, as in this example that points up the dog-of-a-life led by a newsvendor.

Along the same lines, sometimes the use of simile and metaphor can be used to cause a punchline effect. In "La vita in campagna" (*RR*) the protagonist must, against his will, spend some time in the country. A friend tries to dissuade him: "Ma con chi farai paino? Con le vacche? Con i maiali?" (296). When he arrives at his host's home in the country, the classic "farmer's daughter" is "robusta . . . due fianchi di cavallo. Gente addirittura simile agli animali . . ." (298). Once the animal imagery is well established, we get the rest of the joke: "E lei invece mi pareva proprio una vacca. 'Fai, fai' pensavo, 'tu di certo vacca sei . . . ma io non sarò il toro'" (299). In this story the woman-animal connection seems less important than the set-up for the final one-liner. Nevertheless, she is compared to an animal, as we have seen so often with other women in this study. Further, her being linked to a passive animal (*vacca*) allows the protagonist to project himself as the unwilling aggressor (*toro*); woman is adjunct to man.[2]

A different sort of twist occurs in "Donna cavallo" (*Un'altra vita*). The female protagonist hears herself called a *cavallona* and begins to think about the attribution.

> Guardandomi, la parola "cavallona" mi torna alla mente e non posso fare a meno di riconoscerne la verità. Sono infatti molto alta con le spalle larghe e il bacino largo; ma ho le gambe lunghe, agili e magre; e, nell'insieme, la grande macchina femminile del mio corpo dà un'impressione di armonia e persino di eleganza. Appunto come i cavalli che sono i soli animali ad essere al tempo stesso grandi e graziosi. Purtroppo, anche la mia faccia ossuta è cavallina, con la fronte molto bassa, il naso lungo e la bocca prominente. Ma soprattutto i miei occhi fanno pensare a quelli di un cavallo. Rotondi, neri, limpidi, rivelano tuttavia una folle inquietudine in fondo alla loro limpidezza. Mi domando a questo punto se lo sconosciuto passante dicendomi "cavallona", abbia voluto farmi un complimento. E decido che si è limitato a descrivermi. Sì, è così, sono una "cavallona", una ragazza che se si fosse sposata, chissà, forse, sarebbe adesso semplicemente una matrona; e che, invece, restando nubile, è diventata pian piano la caricatura di se stessa e ha finito per rassomigliare ad un animale. L'idea del cavallo mi torna a tavola, poco dopo. Mio padre allunga una mano per farmi una carezza e io ho subito uno scarto violento con il capo, proprio come un cavallo. Mia madre mi nomina d'improvviso: "Rossana", e io, al mio nome, faccio un salto, appunto come un cavallo che si adombra. (*Un'altra vita* 185)

This passage seems quite remarkable in many respects, not the least important of which is that it is the rare woman who would

---

[2] In her introduction to *The Female Body in Western Culture*, Susan Suleiman observes that certain problems for women arise over and over again in our culture: "Having power versus lacking it, speaking versus keeping silent, acting versus supporting action, existing for oneself, as subject, versus existing for the other as object" (3).

write it, describing herself in ways that interpret the term *cavallona* as connoting anything remotely approximating *armonia* and *eleganza*. One is usually unaware that one's own eyes "fanno pensare a" anything. That the woman would then go on to agree ("Sì, è così, sono una "cavallona") is equally difficult to fathom; and why would a *single* woman become a "caricature of herself" to eventually resemble an animal, when the same woman if *married* would merely become a matron? Moravia seems erroneously to be creating for this female character a kind of displacement of self-image; people simply do not see themselves in these ways.[3] The self-description does not sound authentic; it brings up the question of whether he could ever have succeeded at all in writing convincingly like a woman. Wood believes that "When a male reader takes over a female narrating voice, he defines not only her experience but his own, her experience as he perceives, understands and names it" (79).[4] But Wood implies that the author has indeed "defined" the woman's experience (along with his own); in the case of the *cavallona*, this may not be true. It is debatable whether anyone's experience (but his own) is represented here.

Returning to the *cavallona*, after several other equine movements, the protagonist finds herself in heavy traffic.

> Tra tutte queste macchine, ecco, incede una vecchia carrozza di piazza, col suo cavallo. Com'è strano il cavallo tra tutte quelle automobili! Com'è singolare il suo corpo grande e grosso sulle quattro gambe sottili! E come si vede che "morde il freno", inquieto, incapace di inserirsi nel traffico meccanizzato! Lo guardo affascinata e fraterna. La parola "cavallona" evidentemente continua ad agire. Mi dico che sono "matta come un cavallo"; e pur

---

[3] Carol Gilligan writes that "When the observer is a woman, the perspective may be of a different sort" (5).

[4] Sharon Wood continues: "The problem is not simply that Moravia cannot write like a woman, however that may be, or that the first person narrators are women while the author is a man. It is, rather, that the stories consistently fail to find a sufficient means of expression of personal, subjective experience. Rather than unite body and mind, Eros and Logos, in the act of writing, they drive a further wedge between the two. The narrators are subject to a schizophrenia with linguistic and narrative rather than social and cultural origins; while they relate their own stories, they are similtaneously turned into objects by the text itself" (82-83). "The women are not in control of the text, but are, rather, seen by it. Self-preservation becomes not a matter of shared experience but of inviting external observation; the women become not the subject but the object of the text" (86).

> guardando alla carrozza che si allontana pian piano tra le mac-
> chine, comincio a piangere, ritta in piedi contro il davanzale,
> sporgendo le labbra ad afferrare le lagrime, appunto come un
> cavallo sporge la bocca ad afferrare la zolla di zucchero. (190)

The passage completes the original "set-up" in that we find out why Moravia constructed her as a horse – to then compare her with the incongruity of an animal in automobile traffic, a square peg in a round hole, a fish out of water. She realizes her dilemma and cries (before reaffirming her own identity as an animal licking her own tears).

This is a particularly clumsy use of extended imagery in a not particularly well-written short story, but it does illustrate well a tentative, lengthy orchestration of imagery. Important as well is the (unbelievable) fact that this *cavallona* is also made to be fully aware of and in agreement with her animal-status in life, even to such an extent that she lives the part to the maximum, allowing it to color her entire self-perception.

Imagery on a more extended level appears in the short story "Ladri in chiesa" (*Racconti romani,* p. 260). The protagonist, who has a wife and three children, is unemployed; they live in a cave in the outskirts of Rome, and have nothing to eat. In desperation, he and his wife decide to rob a church. Moravia's sustained use of wolf-imagery represents a step in the evolution of his use of metaphor as an important instrument in his stylistic orchestrations to highlight his political views:

> Che fa il lupo quando la lupa e i lupetti hanno fame e stanno a
> pancia vuota, lamentandosi e bisticciandosi tra loro, che fa il
> lupo? Io dico che il lupo esce dalla tana e va in cerca di roba da
> mangiare e magari, dalla disperazione, scende al paese ed entra
> in una casa. E i contadini che l'ammazzano hanno ragione di am-
> mazzarlo; ma anche lui ha ragione e il torto non ce l'ha nessuno;
> e dalla ragione nasce la morte. Quell'inverno io ero come il lupo
> e, anzi, proprio come un lupo non abitavo in una casa ma in una
> grotta, laggiù, sotto Monte Mario, in una cava abbandonata di
> pozzolana (260).

The protagonist first sets out the problem in wolfly terms. The metaphoric distancing allows Moravia to add a political note about class struggle without seeming to intrude or to ascend a pulpit of his own: everyone is right and "il torto non ce l'ha nessuno." This pronouncement put into the mouth of the man-wolf seems quite logical. He extends the metaphor even further. ". . . e leggevo in quegli otto occhi (his family) la stessa espressione affamata, mi pareva proprio di essere un lupo con una famiglia di lupi . . ." (261), and in so doing he also extends the seriousness of his political views. A desperate man must provide for his wife and children, and (implicitly) it does not matter how.

The protagonist puts his plan into effect; they set out for Rome. "Proprio come due lupi affamati che scendono dal monte al paese; e chiunque, vedendoci, ci avrebbe preso per due lupi" (262). He circles like a wolf ". . . presi a girare per la chiesa senza sapere che fare" (263). Finally, he thinks it over, and falls asleep instead. His plan is aborted, but the lupine imagery has fueled the short story throughout; and it has allowed the author to make a political statement without being heavy handed.

Moravia also uses imagistic orchestrations to suggest a kind of psychological displacement. For example, in the short story entitled "La moglie-giraffa" (*La villa del venerdì*) Riccardo, a jealous husband, is in the jungle looking at giraffes. He immediately thinks of his wife, Gigliola, who physically resembles a giraffe: "le gambe straordinarie, massicce nella parte superiore, sottili nella parte inferiore, e lui allora pensava indispettito: 'Una giraffa, nient'altro che una sciocca giraffa'" (168). He takes out his rifle and shoots at one of the animals. Later within earshot of his mother-in-law, he confesses to his wife that he tried to kill a giraffe when he thought of her. The mother-in-law takes him aside and points out that he has clearly threatened Gigliola, the *sciocca giraffa*. "Come se avesse detto: 'ieri è toccata alla giraffa, domani a te'" (171).

The reader probably does not need the mother-in-law's analysis of Riccardo's mental substitutions to understand what is happening in this story. The example illustrates, however, one of the ways in which Moravia orchestrates imagery to give a (crude) psychological twist to the story. He calls on animal imagery (at the wife's expense) ostensibly to describe Gigliola, when he really is talking about the social taboo of uxoricide.

We can only conclude from these renditions of women that besides being the "Other," the fragmented, and the ungraspable, in the preceeding examples they are also functional, as food and as animals; women underscore certain thematic ideas. What is disturbing is that the points are made with such ease and nonchalance. In the case of the examples concerning men, the newsagent as dog and the man as wolf are constructed for the purpose of correcting a socio-political wrong. Life inside a newspaper kiosk is a dog's life; a man reduced to desperation is like a wolf. We must forgive him and understand him. Never is there the suggestion of shooting him (as Riccardo does to Gigliola's metaphorical vehicle), or undervaluing him like a loaf of bread, or mistreating him like a beast.

The most sustained and imagistically dense example of "simple orchestration" (without ever reaching the stylistic heights that will be seen later in *La ciociara*), occurs in the novel *La mascherata* where the imagery is consistently animalesque, but where, on the other hand, Moravia never actually exploits its narrative possibilities. *La mascherata* is a short novel of political and emotional intrigue, treason, double crossings, fanatic idealism and power, appropriately set in a fictitious Latin American country which is suspiciously similar to Fascist Italy. Moravia depicts a society in terms of beast-levels, and presents a culture via a quasi-allegory of the Duce's political society.

The short novel is rife with imagery of (men) hunting and dog imagery (females), of lions (men) and their victims (women), masters and their pets (both men and women). The dictator, General Tereso Arango, is forever hunting Fausta.[5] Fausta accepts his invitation to go to his *hunting* lodge. Sebastiano, also in love with Fausta ". . . come un giovane leone che strascichi la vittima ancor viva dentro la tana per divorarsela a tutto il suo agio, si era diretto trascinando Fausta" (46). Sebastiano *da cacciatore* whistles for Fausta under her window. She hears him and we see her teeth: "i canini bianchi e aguzzi, la mandibola grossa e tonda di gatto" (48). Meanwhile the *maggiordomo* wonders if Saverio and Sebastiano are "cani o preda" (63).

We see a woman's face "in tutto simile al muso di un cane pechinese: (. . .) naso rincagnato." Fausta's door opens and the maid "dal naso rincagnato" appears. Her eyes are "spiritati di cane." Sebastiano points toward Fausta's door and asks whose it is.

---

[5] The general's name, Tereso Arango, is suspiciously close both to Doroteo Arango, alias Pancho Villa, and in sound to the first person, singular of the Spanish verb *arañar*, to scratch or claw. Although one would not want to make more than a passing reference to the linguistic resemblance of *araño* and *arango*, the well chosen name is conveniently close in tone to the general's personality.

" 'Caccia riservata' rispose la donna crudamente" (68), indicating that they know well the metaphoric ground rules: they are all animals and it is hunting season.

Tereso hopes that a beautiful woman will heel at his feet. Other women arrive; they also take the order to heel. Tereso refers to Fausta as a *brutta bestia*. Fausta strains at her leash. The duchess treats the maid, Giustina (*faccia di cagnolino*) *da bestia*: "hai proprio una faccia in tutto simile al muso di un cane" (98-99). Fausta and Doroteo (a golf caddie) make an especially interesting pair of lovers: Fausta kneels next to him and ruffles his hair. She calls him tenderly *bestia*. When she gets tired of him she will throw him out "come un cane (. . .) ti farò bastonare" (113).

All through the story the characters sniff each other out, have a *fiuto* for one thing or another, sense the *odore* of treachery. They heel to their master; they are on leashes. They show their fangs; they do just about everything with great *accanimento*. The men are a combination of hunters, dog-trainers whose bitches heel at their feet, lions, and beasts to be beaten. The women are hunters' prey, on leashes, cats, dogs, beasts and puppy-faced idiots.

Unfortunately, this elaborate dog/beast construction is never used for anything but what eventually becomes overly-done description. It fails to evolve as a functioning, informing component of the plot. In fact, it could be argued that the very first example cited in this chapter is much more sophisticated: that of the bread-faced wife in "Un dritto" where imagery serves a more important role than all the examples regarding the *Mascherata* (and only a few are mentioned here). In the bread-wife example, if we do not make the wife/bread connection, we cannot understand the husband's boredom with homemade bread. In the much more imagistically intense *La mascherata*, however, about all that the dog/beast imagery tells us is that the characters, in particular the women, are animals.

In his attempts to make imagery serve an orchestrated role in his prose, Moravia uses it to convey a punchline, as a means of rationalization or psychological displacement of socially proscribed behavior, and at times for pure play. Sometimes he can be clumsy with this instrument ("Donna cavallo"); he can be political; and, he can also fail completely, where in *La mascherata* one senses that he wanted to do something with that abundance of sustained imagery, but never quite succeeded.

Imagery is a poetic evasion; it speaks of "other things," to go back to its etymology. Imagery transmits messages symbolically. Rudimentary and conventional as these examples may be, they illustrate a deliberate phenomenon in Moravia's works – describing characters with images, and then attempting to make those metaphors and similes pivotal to the plot structure. Without some awareness of the centrality of metaphor, we cannot fully understand the story. In *La ciociara,* however, Moravia takes this technique a quantum leap beyond the use of imagery discussed above where the similes and metaphors in most instances do enrich the writing, but carry few serious thematic implications.

V

COMPLEX ORCHESTRATION OF IMAGERY

> We have now seen that, on the contrary, poetic
> metaphor, far from being ornamentation, deals with
> central and indispensable aspects of our conceptual
> system.
>
> (Lakoff and Turner 215)

In *La ciociara* Moravia first provides omens and premonitions
throughout the narrative to prepare the reader for the tragedies to
come for the mother and daughter protagonists, Cesira and Rosetta.
At the same time and just as consistently, he individualizes the
daughter through imagery both as a sacrificial lamb and scapegoat
who is bound for tragedy. She is described repeatedly with these
principal similes and metaphors so that at a certain point in the
novel with each reference to lamb-like or goat-like qualities, we automatically think of Rosetta. Eventually the mere mention of "lambness" or "goatness" becomes a literary shorthand telling the reader
that something regarding Rosetta is about to happen; the result is
an automatic link between omen and image whenever anything
ovine or caprine is stated. Moravia prepares in us a predictable response; we are stylistically conditioned for the ultimate tragedy. The
descriptive package of imagery assigned to Rosetta forms certain
patterns; it underlines her type of character, and it allows her to
take part logically with other characters and in scenes of the novel
in a way which would seem otherwise contrived. Above all, it gives
Rosetta a moral role to play within the grand scheme of the novel.
Although narrative omens and premonitions are common to writers
from the Greek classics to the moderns and are not at all peculiar to

Moravia, he uses them in this novel to enhance the recurrent imagery of sacrifice and expiation, thus orchestrating his ensemble of stylistic devices in an unusually complex way.

In this chapter I plan to discuss Moravia's blending of omen with his imagistic presentation of Rosetta. I will identify and analyze his metaphors and similes in order to determine patterns or types. Then I will examine the dependence of theme on imagery and vice versa. I hope to elucidate the associative functions (i.e., linking acts, events and individuals) of imagistic expression as well as its immediate descriptive function.

It is World War II; the Allies are pushing north from Naples toward Rome; the widowed Cesira and her teenage daughter, Rosetta, leave Rome, still held by the Nazis, and go south to the hills of Ciociaria to sit out the winter away from the main theatre of action. Thinking it safe to return, after a trying stay in the mountains and a series of adventures, they are sexually assaulted by a squad of Moroccan soldiers sent to aid the Allies. They are left to deal with the aftermath of emotional and physical upheaval as well as with the denouement of the war.

The first person narrator, Cesira, begins her story with a feeling of anxiety as she fills her narrative details with foreboding. She tells the story in retrospect: ". . . e non sapevo che proprio a Roma mi aspettava la disgrazia" (5). She tells us of her presages: ". . . ma nello stesso tempo avevo non so che presentimento non soltanto di un'assenza più lunga ma anche di qualche cosa di triste che mi aspettasse nell'avvenire. . . . avevo paura ma non sapevo di che" (24-25). Yet, at the beginning she remains vague about the exact nature of her sense of doom; she builds tension with her general feelings of impending tragedy.

Moravia blends Cesira's own naive prediction that the future will be fine with the omen of a siren portending an as-yet-unknown future event. Ironically she tells Rosetta that all this bombing will pass, the war will end, scarcities will disappear, Rosetta will get married and live happily ever after: "Proprio in quel momento, come per darmi una risposta, ecco suonare la sirena d'allarme, quel rumore maledetto che mi pareva che portasse iettatura e mi faceva ogni volta sprofondare il cuore" (27). Contrasting with her previous feelings expressed in generalizations, now her presentiments are connected directly to her daughter; she is less vague about her pre-monitions.[1]

As Rosetta and Cesira wend their way south to Ciociaria they spend some time at the home of the treacherous Concetta, who re-assures the mother of her daughter's safety: "Tua figlia qui sta sicura come in chiesa" (65). These seemingly kind and simple words are loaded with hidden meaning. Concetta's simile predicts the place of the eventual rape, *in chiesa*. Later Cesira even dreams of Rosetta's church wedding (336). Moravia tightens the links of omens; he makes them depend upon each other as he focuses sharply on Rosetta as the victim of this unknown future event.[2]

Then in a *tour de force* of transpositional imagery, Moravia uses Cesira's description of the Allied shelling in the sky as a shadow im-age of the horror of the physical violence to come for herself and her daughter: "Queste tracce rosse parevano proprio rasoiate nel cielo, *con il sangue che sgorgava un momento dalle ferite e poi subito cessava. Vedevamo dapprima la rasoiata: quindi ci arrivava il botto di partenza; subito dopo, udivamo proprio sulle nostre teste un miagolìo arrabbiato e soffiato*; quasi nello stesso tempo . . . giungeva lo scop-pio d'arrivo, fortissimo, che faceva rintronare il cielo come una stan-za vuota" (287; italics mine). Later we will compare this presage with the actual rape, and in retrospect it will take on significance as Moravia's most clear premonitory sign. It is another way of present-ing the rape – the cutting, the blood, the thrust, the orgasm, the fi-nal whimper, followed by the macho *scoppio d'arrivo*. This is a more distant, more removed description of what is to come, but later we will see interesting parallels in diction and syntax with the rape scene. These pseudo-rapes, the shellings, continue to light up the sky as war and rape dovetail.[3] As the description of the shelling ties in with Rosetta's defilement, war becomes analogous to rape, rape

---

[1] In a subsequent scene, Rosetta has heard a gruesome tale of the sexual vio-lence of war. Cesira again assures Rosetta that nothing will happen to her, that all will be fine, that soldiers do not really molest women during wartime, and that, fur-thermore, the two of them are going to the country in Ciociaria and "lì non succe-derà proprio niente, sta 'tranquilla'" (34). This sadly ironic twist shows the progres-sion of the omens, from the general and non-specific to the much more precise.

[2] Moravia uses auditory imagery as well in his recurring cock crowing, and col-or imagery by taking advantage of the ubiquitous "Fascist black," so prevalent in Italy during the "ventennio nero" (see 36; 38; 40; 41; 73).

[3] For an excellent discussion of this use of metaphor and all of its ramifica-tions, see George Lakoff and Mark Johnson, *Metaphors We Live By*.

to war. Thus, a seemingly straightforward image not only portends the future, but helps to describe it. It transforms the novel from the simple story of two victims to the quasi-allegory of two women who are also integral parts of a much larger and more universal meaning, i.e., the violence done to Rosetta is like that done to Italy during the war.

Ominous imagery appears once again when Cesira and Rosetta run at night to escape the bombings. They stumble into a stream, get soaked and muddy, and then awaken after a night in the fields: ". . . e accanto alla mia faccia c'erano gli steli alti e gialli; e tra gli steli alcuni *papaveri di un rosso tanto bello* . . . ."[4] Guardai Rosetta che mi stava distesa accanto e tuttora dormiva; e vidi che aveva il viso tutto *sbaffato di fango nero e secco* e anche *le gambe e la gonna erano nere di fango* fin quasi al ventre . . ." (326; italics mine). This description prefigures the violent scene yet to come. The red of the poppies functions much like the red wake of the shells in the sky of the previous citation, a seconding refrain to imagery of blood. The mud is also a replacement of the blood that will later take its place on her body. After the rape Rosetta returns to a stream of water for cleansing, thus coming full circle by fulfilling this presage of water and mud. Both images here are warnings foreshadowing the violence.

The winter of 1943-44 was abnormally rainy (read muddy). It is logical for Moravia to emphasize mud. For it both reflects in a realistic way the physical hardship of the war experience, and forms a set of recurring images – images created out of the realism of the situation. Bearing this in mind, his insistence on that mud as a convenient image as well as a meteorological fact makes the prose much less contrived than if mud had not been reality that winter.

In one of the last major scenes involving presignification, Cesira describes Rosetta who is in semi-shock over a bombing incident during which their makeshift house was totally destroyed only a short time after their escape. This near-miss has sobered them considerably to the dangers of war, a reality which they had previously ignored. An American soldier approaches her:

---

[4] See the similar use of poppies and the color red, both in Verga's short story, "La Lupa," in Giovanni Verga, *Tutte le novelle* (Milano: Mondadori, 1970), 145; and in Elio Vittorini, *Erica e i suoi fratelli* (Milano: Bompiani, 1956).

... vedendo Rosetta seduta sui sassi, immobile e attontita, sostò a parlarle. Lei non rispondeva e lo guardava; lui prima le parlò in inglese, poi in italiano; alla fine si tolse dalla tasca una sigaretta, gliel'infilò in bocca e se ne andò. E Rosetta restò com'era, con il viso *sbaffato di fango nero e secco* e quella sigaretta in bocca, penzolante dalle labbra che sarebbe stato perfino una cosa comica se non fosse stato soprattutto triste. (328; italics mine)

In a picture of what Rosetta is about to become, Moravia depicts her in the pose of a prostitute. We see the yet naive Rosetta with a cigarette dangling from her mud-caked face, sitting on a rock by the side of the road, as if waiting for the next client. Again and again, there is that emblematic mud which has already appeared on her metaphorical counterpart, the slaughtered goat.

Because of the omens presented heretofore, we have a presentiment of our own that they will be fulfilled for Rosetta. Moravia uses imagery to build into Rosetta's character a series of signs which tie in with the omens to create a tightly woven prose fabric. Moravia's construction of Rosetta as a sacrificial lamb and scapegoat begins with Cesira's first mention of Rosetta's ovine characteristics: "... aveva un viso come di pecorella . . . e la bocca bella e carnosa che sporgeva però sul mento ripiegato, proprio come quella delle pecore. E i capelli ricordavano il pelo degli agnelli . . ." (19). In yet another description of Rosetta's face, Cesira again says that Rosetta's facial characteristics are such ". . . che la faceva rassomigliare un poco ad una pecorella" (166).

They arrive in the mountains and upon seeing their rustic accommodations, Cesira explains that they would have to cook, eat and live in that stall-like hut, ". . . proprio come due capre o due pecore" (102). As Moravia blends and blurs the distinction between lamb and goat, Cesira metaphorizes herself and Rosetta to suggest the scene later when they actually do find goats in a hut – goats whose situation will bear a remarkable resemblance to their own.

Moravia even has Rosetta and Cesira literally consuming the image, perhaps alluding to the religious sacrifice where the word is made flesh and then eaten. For during their stay in the mountains in the evening they usually eat a thin soup and some pieces of meat, ". . . quasi sempre capra, nelle tre varietà della capra femmina, del caprettone e del caprone" (121).

Moravia's choice of lamb/goat for Rosetta eventually becomes not at all inappropriate within the limits of his imagistic orchestration in this novel; the image is not surprising. He has convinced us to accept the metaphor *ad rem*; for his purposes, she *is* a lamb.[5] After hearing a gruesome description of wartime atrocities, Rosetta remarks, "Io, però, preferirei sempre essere tra quelli *che vengono ammazzati* che tra quelli che ammazzano" (141; italics mine). Rosetta has a simple, nun-like attitude, a resignation that will not get her through this war unscarred. In addition, within her words there is the self-image of actually being a sacrificial offering.

In a key passage of predominant caprine imagery, where the goat is about to be slaughtered, Rosetta says:

> Mamma, quella povera capra mi fa compassione . . . ora è viva, tra poco l'ammazzeranno . . . se dipendesse da me, non l'ammazzerei. Le dissi: 'E che mangeresti allora?' Lei rispose: 'Pane e verdura . . . che bisogno c'è di mangiare carne? *Anch'io sono fatta di carne e questa carne di cui sono fatta non è poi tanto diversa dalla carne di questa capra* . . . che colpa ne ha lei se è una bestia e non può ragionare e diffendersi? (178; italics mine)

Ironically, Rosetta's upbringing has rendered her just as incapable of defending herself as the goat of which she speaks.[6] Again she equates herself with the sacrifice by comparing the flesh of the goat to her own. The literal goat will eventually be devoured by the refugees, meat for the masses, just as Rosetta will be consumed by the gang of Moroccans. Further, the killing of the goat is juxtaposed with Rosetta for a crucial reason. *This* is the description of the rape which Moravia would rather attribute to Rosetta's metaphoric forerunner, the goat, for stylistic interest, and, as we will see later, for an intrinsic thematic reason.

> Ma Ignazio si acchiappò con i denti il labbro inferiore e con un colpo solo le cacciò il coltello in gola, fino al manico, *sempre tenendola ferma per le corna*. Filippo, che *gli faceva da aiutante*,

---

[5] In *The Kristeva Reader*, Kristeva alludes to the same thing in her essay "The True Real" ("Le vréel") when she talks about the signifier being taken for the real, or the "concretization" of the signifier.

[6] Consider Cesira's initial description of Rosetta's good upbringing, her sheltered rearing, her good Catholic education, and her religious naiveté (see 112-14).

fu lesto a mettere la catinella sotto la gola della capra; dalla ferita, il sangue colò giù come una fontanella, *nero e denso*, caldo che fumava per l'aria. La capra fremette, *poi chiuse a metà gli occhi che le si erano già appannati come se, a misura che il sangue colava nel catino, la vita se ne fosse andata e con la vita anche lo sguardo*; infine piegò le ginocchia e si abbandonò, si sarebbe detto ancora fiduciosa, tra le mani di colui che l'aveva scannata. Rosetta si era allontanata . . . Ignazio, intanto aveva sollevato la capra per le zampe di dietro e, *strascinandola per il fango*, era andato ad appenderla a due pali, poco più in là, testa in giù e *zampe larghe*. Insomma, lui, piano piano, tolse via tutta la pelle e poi la gettò in terra, pelosa e sanguinolenta, *simile ad un vestito smesso*; e *adesso la capra era nuda*, per così dire, tutta rossa con *qualche chiazza bianca* e bluastra qua e là. (179-80; italics mine)

This passage functions exactly as did the omen where the description of the shelling is a veiled pictorial image of the physical effects of rape. Here instead we have the bloody scene literally, while the shelling scene is slightly more in the abstract. This instance presents a factual killing and represents progression from the general to the specific, not unlike that of the evolution of the presages as reported by Cesira at the beginning of the novel. The logical conclusion of this crescendo effect is a sense of the impending violence against Rosetta herself. We know it is coming. Moravia has conditioned us by linking all of these diverse images to each other, and each in turn to Rosetta. He simply strikes his image key to suggest a whole ensemble of interrelated pictures, colors, textures and sounds. In this goat-slaughter Moravia tightens up even more on his image strings where they all come to bear on the actual plot. It is here at this high, climactic point where his style is simply inseparable from what is happening within the story.

It is significant that the rape itself is not reported in anything but literal terms. Moravia is confident that we *know* and *saw* the gruesome scene before it happened through our associations in the shelling scene and in the goat slaughter scene. In this way he keeps intact the essential link between the scapegoat and Rosetta. It means, as well, that he already has described through imagery what Cesira, having been beaten unconscious by the Moroccans, cannot have actually seen. In place of a description by Cesira, Moravia provides the shelling, the goat-slaughter, and the rape scenes. All three as one provide a total depiction of the event. The first two are omen and analogy to the third. Together they blend into a picture that equals more than the sum of its parts.

In the actual, climactic rape scene Cesira and Rosetta are trapped in a deserted church by a group of Moroccans. There ensues a violent scene of gang rape; the soldiers leave them sprawled on the floor of the church and go on their way. The desperate Cesira looks at Rosetta:

> *L'avevano trascinata* o lei era fuggita fin sotto l'altare; stava distesa, supina, *con le vesti rialzate* sopra la testa che non si vedeva, *nuda dalla vita ai piedi. Le gambe erano rimaste aperte* come loro l'avevano lasciate, e si vedeva *il ventre bianco* come il marmo e il pelo biondo e ricciuto simile alla testina *di un capretto* e sulla parte interna delle cosce, *c'era del sangue* e ce n'era anche sul pelo. Io pensai che fosse morta anche per via del sangue il quale, benché capissi che era il sangue della sua verginità massacrata, era pur sangue e suggeriva idee di morte. (. . .) Vidi, allora che lei mi guardava *con occhi spalancati, senza dir parola né muoversi, con uno sguardo che non le avevo mai visto, come di animale che sia stato preso in trappola e non può muoversi e aspetta che il cacciatore* gli dia l'ultimo colpo. (352; italics mine)

With just a few brushstrokes, Moravia calls us back to what we have already seen in the goat-slaughter.[7] Compare my italicized phrases of the goat-slaughter with those of the actual rape. Moroccan accomplices hold her down just as the goat's butcher, Ignazio, has his assistant, Filippo, to hold down the animal. There is the goat with her *zampe larghe* and here are Rosetta's *gambe aperte*. The

---

[7] In *Io e lui* the character, Irene, in her fantasy masturbation sees herself as an animal to be butchered. "Beh, nel mio secondo film immaginavo di essere una di quelle giovanette ingrassate apposta per essere mangiate. Mi piaceva, insomma, l'idea di non essere che un animale domestico, da carne, di quelli che, appunto, si fanno a pezzi e si vendono sui marmi delle macellerie." She narrates the fantasy-masturbation film: "Il cuoco entrava, mi palpava ben bene per vedere se ero grassa a punto, quindi mi afferrava per i capelli e mi sgozzava tenendomi la gola su un secchio per raccogliere il sangue. Dopo di che, mi appendeva per i piedi, a testa in giù, e mi squartava con la mannaia, cominciando dall'inguine, lungo tutta la colonna vertebrale, fino al collo. Così avevo visto fare ad un maiale, in campagna. Dalla cucina, poi, nel mio film, passavo subito alla tavola. Vedevo un grande vassoio collocato nel mezzo della tavola e sul vassoio c'ero io, le mie mani, la mia testa, le mie gambe e così via, tutti confusi e mischiati, come appunto i pezzi di un animale cucinato" (104). As well, in *La romana* the female protagonist is in her room with the brutish Sonzogno. "A quel modo, non potei fare a meno di pensare, si preparano negli ospedali i chirurghi, accingendosi a qualche sanguinosa operazione. O peggio i beccai, sotto gli occhi stessi del capretto che debbono sgozzare" (208).

goat's half-closed, clouded eyes lose their vivacity along with the life that drains from its body; Rosetta has the terrified eyes of a trapped animal waiting for death. She was trapped in the church, just as the omen suggested. The goat gives herself over "fiduciosa tra le mani di colui che l'aveva scannata," just as Rosetta waits for the death blow: ". . . come un agnello che viene condotto al macello e non lo sa e lecca la mano che lo trascina verso il coltello" (335). In the aftermath of rape, just as the Moroccans toss Rosetta aside nude, blood stained and brutalized, Filippo tosses away the goat's skin, leaving the animal nude, red-stained with a few images of bruises here and there. If there were *any* doubt that the goat-slaughter *is* the rape scene (i.e., that the omen *is* the image), one would need only to note that Rosetta's pubic area is "simile alla testina di un capretto." In retrospect Cesira even calls the rape scene *quel macello* (369), a term used quite often in colloquial Roman speech. In this case, *macello* clearly takes on extra meaning beyond and apart from its everyday usage. Gian Paolo Biasin has noted: "Non sorprenderà notare che a questo punto Rosetta incarna la similitudine che le si riferisce attraverso tutto il romanzo, diventando letteralmente il *capro espiatorio* della violenza della guerra: l'altare e la chiesa sembrano sottolineare il carattere rituale e sacrale dell'azione, mentre a un altro livello l'azione stessa sconsacra, desacralizza il luogo in cui è compiuta" (60).

Moravia's constant allusion to the scapegoat has caused in turn an equally constant connection to Rosetta which gets produced eventually by the mental agility of the reader, not even necessarily by the author in his text.

While the goat's blood runs *nero e denso*, Rosetta's sticks to her pubic hair, recalling not only the violence but the leitmotif of prefiguring mud, *nero e secco*, throughout the narrative – both in relation to the muddy, dead goat and to her previous experiences with muddy face and legs. The development of the motif has been first the scene of mud on the goat, then mud on her face and legs, and now blood in place of mud after the rape. While watching the goat being slaughtered, Rosetta was up to her ankles in mud. Mud is as common as death and destruction in a story about war, especially in Italy during that particularly wet season,[8] but in the case of this

---

[8] At the beginning of the novel Cesira was describing the difficulty of living even a base existence in the mountains in a one-room hut with pounded earth for a floor (see 171; 173; 178).

novel, it is also of metaphoric significance; so, in rereading the novel even non-representational mud means more to us. It prefigures the time when it *will* mean something. Mud is not just negative, but literally a real impediment to the protagonists' existence. Therefore, it is also the most appropriate image to prefigure the blood on Rosetta's legs after the rape, since Moravia did not even have to invent it *ad rem*. In the aftermath, Cesira takes charge of Rosetta, who is in a stupor. She eventually finds a shepherd's hut in which to stay. Approaching it they hear goats bleating. Cesira describes them as "quando stanno al buio e vogliono uscire" (357). Cesira has to dethatch the hut to get to the goats: ". . . e tosto, come ebbi allargato il buco, una capra bianca e nera ci affacciò la testa, mettendo le zampe sul muro, guardandomi con i suoi occhi d'oro e belando appena. Io le dissi: 'Su, bella, salta, salta; ma vidi che lei, poveretta, con tutto che cercasse di tirarsi su non ne aveva la forza e capii che quelle capre erano indebolite dal digiuno e che bisognava che le tirassi fuori io' " (357).

This scene might initially appear as a relief from the heavily dramatic rape scene, but Moravia is, in fact, allegorically describing (1) the two women trapped in the church, screaming like the bleating goats, and (2) less literally Cesira's attempts to draw Rosetta out of her *abulia*, her being in the dark and wanting to get out just like the goats, and perhaps even being *bianca e nera* like the goat. (See the description of Rosetta immediately after the rape: *il ventre bianco* and the blood/mud running *nero e denso*.) Unfortunately Rosetta does not have the instinct for survival that Cesira has, or even that the goats have. Her mother has provided an overly sheltered upbringing; Rosetta was educated by the nuns to be naive; yet, ironically she was defiled in the church.

Cesira enters the hut and finds a supine mother goat with a kid at her side: "Io pensai che questa capra giacesse così immobile per far poppare il capretto ma, poiché mi fui avvicinata, vidi che la capra, invece, era morta" (358). Is this perhaps a sign of her own inability to help her daughter? Or is Cesira dead in another way, as Michele, the novel's moral conscience, has repeatedly suggested? Continuing the extended metaphor, Moravia provides a ray of hope for the future. Cesira puts the kids outside to pasture: ". . . si udivano i loro belati; sempre più chiari e sempre più forti, come se, ad ogni boccone, la voce gli si fosse riaffermata e quelle povere bestie avessero voluto farmi sentire che stavano meglio e che mi ringraziavano di averle salvate dalla morte per fame" (358). Just as the baby goats devour the food they find upon their liberation from the hut, Rosetta's appetite as well reveals itself to be nothing short of voracious.

Cesira must also release Rosetta, just as she did the kids, in order to find her own solution, to grow strong on her own. Her sheltered rearing has ill-served her to cope with this emotional trauma. Cesira must give her the independence to work it out by herself. How can we interpret this scene otherwise? What function could it have?[9] Later in another analogy with Rosetta, Cesira points out that the goats have abandoned their dead mother (just as Cesira is dead for Rosetta, and unable to help her) and now take their nourishment elsewhere: ". . . i capretti che avevano ricominciato a poppare ora da una ora dall'altra di esse e già si erano del tutto dimenticati della madre morta. Rosetta era sempre dello stesso umore, apatico, indifferente, distante . . ." (362). Even syntactically the goats and Rosetta are juxtaposed. Rosetta will indeed abandon her mother to try to make sense of her experience elsewhere. Cesira and Rosetta stay at the hut for four nights during which "Le capre . . . tornavano per conto loro alla capanna . . ." (362). This reference to their new independence is meant also to predict Rosetta's own rebellious and licentious behavior in the next few days, when she too will come and go as she pleases.

In one final allusion to Rosetta as the sacrificial scapegoat Moravia introduces the truck driver who will shortly become Rosetta's lover. "Aveva la voce grossa a rauca; sul collo enorme gli ricadevano tanti riccioletti biondi che gli facevano *una testa come di caprone; e aveva veramente qualche cosa del caprone nel modo con il quale guardava Rosetta*" (367-68; italics mine). Rosetta has found her metaphoric mate; and he even offers her caprine gifts! "Ti piacerebbe un bel taglio di lana per un vestito? O un bel paio di scarpe di capretto?" (368).

Because of Moravia's use of imagery in this novel, Rosetta is not reducible to literal statements. Felicity Haynes has said: "On the comparative level we are transferring characteristics of Y to X in order to say something about X. On the interactive level, placing known characteristics of Y against those of X may provide *new* in-

---

[9] Note the identical allegorical use of the "James" movie scene in Vasco Pratolini, *Il quartiere*, 153-54.

sights, either about X or about a new third, Z, an irreducible synthesis by juxtaposition which it is difficult to reduce to simile or to
literal language" (273). Something more is created with that "irreducible synthesis." Rosetta is not merely the sum of her parts. Out
of simple comparison with lowly animals, there results a whole
third image of her. It is difficult to describe literally this new cre-
ation by paraphrasing the instances of its development, but she
emerges as a much rounder character with Moravia's evocations of
sensory experience through well-chosen words. "No literal paraphrase or statement of similarities will capture the cognitive insight
provided by the metaphor . . . . It would be more illuminating in
some cases to say that the metaphor *creates* the similarity than to say
that it formulates some similarity antecedently existing" (Black 273-
94). Rosetta and her metaphorical equivalents (lambs/goats) merge
and forge a new, third meaning within our minds: what butchers do
to animals, what hunters do to prey, what people do to people, nations to nations – it is all the same: violence. As such, it carries the
same painful ramifications.

Although I have adopted a deliberately artificial separation of
the categories of omen and imagery, it is basic to remember that the
referential instances analyzed are mixed throughout the text and
are cleverly nested and sometimes even deeply imbedded within the
flow of the plot. His style is so refined that only with the closest of
readings can one extrapolate the importance of the individual com-
ponents of Moravia's stylistic devices. Moravia is a painter with
words. He presents colors (red and black) that call to each other
from one part of the narrative to another; textures and substances
(mud and blood) appear and reappear – never gratuitously, always
stylistically functional; sounds echo each other (sirens, cocks crowing); similes and metaphors blur into a tangled web of imagery;
omens dovetail and become metaphors of themselves.

Moravia uses imagery in a highly sophisticated way to bring
Rosetta to the foreground of both her immediate surroundings and
of the general drama of the war. In his search for hidden likenesses,
Moravia's image-izations bear their fruit with our fuller understanding of Rosetta, who otherwise could have been a very flat character.
It is clear that Moravia does not use imagery merely to describe but
to make associative links between acts, events and individuals
throughout the novel. The to-and-fro of omen and image permeates
the narration. Moravia goes to great lengths to develop such an in-

ternal structure. Characteristically he is a very visual narrator. He agrees perhaps that "the mind shuts off at the loss of pictures" (Romano 9). He most certainly wants Rosetta to be the most vivid of the characters. Why?

In *La ciociara*, imagery is a major conveyor of the themes of expiation and sacrifice as embodied in the animal imagery. Imagery gives structural interdependence to theme and style. Although his use of metaphor and simile is in no way as intricately interwoven as Pratolini's, for example, Moravia nevertheless assigns it a crucial function: to make Rosetta part of a stylistic dependency upon her mother (most clearly evident in the scene with the kid goats in the hut). The figurative and the literal are one for Moravia. His style is so galvanized to the story line that we cannot separate the implicit meaning of the lamb/goat imagery from the actual symbolic scene of Cesira's helping the animals literally. We cannot comprehend the allegory without knowing Rosetta's image-ization. To paraphrase I. A. Richards as quoted in the introduction to this study, this is an instance where meaning "is not attainable" without the interaction of tenor and vehicle. Without Rosetta's becoming a sacrificial animal, the meaning of the novel is lost. We would understand nothing about the enmeshed fictional relationship between Rosetta and Cesira. Metaphor and simile are part of a larger plan to reinforce a basic theme of expiation. Moravia is suggesting that Cesira must offer up her firstborn to pay for her sin of indifference to the war, of being dead to human suffering. For Moravia, the middle-class indifference and deliberate ignorance of the moral implications of war are unforgivable. This sin is exemplified by the shopkeeper, Cesira, who thought that she could sit back for the duration and that the war would never touch her personally. Time after time, especially at the beginning of the novel, Cesira states her indifference to the war.

> È vero che c'era la guerra, ma io della guerra non sapevo nulla, siccome non avevo che quella figlia, non me ne importava nulla. S'ammazzassero pure quanto volevano, con gli aeroplani, con i carri armati, con le bombe, a me mi bastava il negozio e l'appartamento per essere felice, come infatti ero. (. . .) Tedeschi, inglesi, americani, russi, per me, come dice il proverbio, ammazza ammazza, è tutta una razza. Ai militari che venivano a bottega e dicevano: vinceremo là, andremo qua, diventeremo, faremo, io gli rispondevo: per me tutto va bene finché il negozio va bene. (10)

Cesira admits to her own profiteering from the war, which she considered a boon to her economic status: ". . . sempre più facevo la borsa nera con prezzi d'affezione, sempre meno vendevo al negozio coi prezzi fissati dal governo" (12). In fact, she even hoped that the war would last to give herself time to amass even more. She would always tell Rosetta to pray that the war would continue a couple more years: ". . . tu allora non soltanto ti fai la dote e il corredo ma diventi ricca" (14). She describes her own indifference as having developed to the point where she did not even care who led the government as long as she could continue her blackmarket activities: "Per me Mussolini o Badoglio o un altro, poco importa, purché si faccia il negozio" (15).

Rosetta exists thematically to function as the *capro espiatorio* for her mother and those like her, blind to the moral ramifications of war. Although the two images, caprine and ovine, evolve along the same stylistic lines, it is important to explore the idea of *why* Rosetta's "lambness" receives slightly less stylistic attention than her more developed "goatness." Why is she more a scapegoat in the dominant scenes of this type of metaphoricity? It is because her mother's blindness and her Lazarus-like death need redemption. Anyone who has reservations about this biblical connection should also consider Cesira's "climb" to the purgatorial mountain of Sant'Eufemia for her spiritual education at the hands of Michele. It is important that whenever she descends that mountain, bad things happen to her.

Rosetta is Abraham's Isaac. Yet Rosetta can stand on her own as a bona fide "round" character in the novel, because of her new self-awareness (unfortunately induced by the brutality of the rape itself). The violence done to Rosetta and its aftermath are turned to good as they help her finally to understand and overcome adversity, where previously she was a sheltered, one-dimensional figure. Dominique Fernandez observes (even if somewhat insensitively), "L'esperienza del sesso si confonde con un'esperienza cosmica, ancestrale della natura, e fa di Rosetta un essere umano completo, compiuto, in armonia con l'universo, gli altri e se stesso, il cui desiderio di gioire non sarà oramai niente altro che la sete di gustare la profusa ricchezza del mondo" (92).

One of the most influential characters, in fact, is Michele who constantly berates the various characters for their deliberate moral blindness to the implications of war, a blindness which results in their being "dead."

... ricordatevi questo: ciascuno di voi è Lazzaro ... e io leggen-
do la storia di Lazzaro ho parlato di voi, di tutti voi ... di te Cesira, di te Rosetta ... siete tutti morti, siamo tutti morti e cre-
diamo di essere vivi ... finché crederemo di essere vivi, perché ci
abbiamo le nostre stoffe, le nostre paure, i nostri affarucci, le
nostre famiglie, i nostri figli, saremo morti, stramorti, putrefatti,
decomposti e che puzziamo di cadavere lontano un miglio,
soltanto allora incominceremo ad essere appena appena vivi ...
Buonanotte. (163-64)

Perhaps the key line of the novel is uttered by Michele in reference to someone else in this particular instance, but it applies
equally well to Cesira. "Finché non perderanno tutto, non capiran-
no niente ... debbono perdere tutto e soffrire e piangere lacrime di
sangue ... soltanto allora saranno maturi" (159). Cesira is guilty of
grave sins to be expiated. In part Michele exists in this novel to
point them up and to underline what Cesira has already admitted
about herself regarding her indifference and greed. *La ciociara* is
the story of Cesira's journey from blindness and death to enlight-
enment and rebirth. She is that dead mother goat; she is Lazarus;
she pays for her sins through tears and pain; and eventually she is
brought back to life through her daughter's song of moral reawak-
ening.

In *La ciociara* imagery serves (1) to describe Rosetta physically,
(2) to blend her psychologically with and pose her against the
omens in imagistic interaction and (3) to offer a stylistic parallel to
reflect the actual progression of the plot. Moravia blends and situates Rosetta and Cesira in imagistic dependency and offers a stylistic reinforcement of the theme, thus offering us a new, less literal
and more allegorical way of seeing the two characters.[10] This figurative play between the two characters makes their *imagistic* dependence as important as their reliance upon each other within the
literal story itself. If I am correct in my reading of this novel,
Moravia's integration of plot with imagery of all types gives us a
seamless unity of style and content, making *La ciociara* technically
one of his most accomplished novels.

---

[10] Moravia, himself, sees the metaphor in allegory as a way to make sense of
"una realtà altrimenti insensata e caotica." Alberto Moravia, "Note sul romanzo,"
L'uomo come fine e altri saggi, 214.

VI

CONCLUSIONS

Da qualche tempo, alcune immagini mi perseguitano.
E' l'iceberg o montagna di ghiaccio galleggiante, che
emerge sulla superficie del mare con poco più che
un'escrescenza, mentre la parte più grande, colossale
chiglia di giaccio glauco, sta sott'acqua, invisibile e in-
sospettata. E' l'orifizio angusto, nascosto dai rovi, os-
truito, introvabile che dà stalagmiti, laghi e fiumi sot-
terranei e saloni e corridoi e passaggi. E' la piccola casa
con una sola porta e una sola finestra, dalla quale si
scende in un'immensa cantina in cui sta chiusa, nera e
lucida, una macchina enorme, che pulsa, batte e ferve.
Le immagini sono molte ma l'idea è pur sempre la stessa: la piccolezza e semplicità di ciò che si vede: l'enor-
mità, potenza e complicazioni di ciò che non si vede.
Ciò che si vede, a dirla in breve è fuori metafora . . ."

(*L'uomo che guarda* 264)

Metaphor and simile are omnipresent in Moravia's fiction,
where imagery can be decorative, discrete, orchestrated, and/or all
of the above, but it is always there. It is more "there" in the existential works, but by no means is it unrepresented in the other works.
Further, Moravia's works considered chronologically do not show
that orchestrated imagery follows necessarily a linear, chronological
progression or evolution into the later works. Over the years from
1929 to his death in 1991, the use of simile and metaphor does not
develope from less sophisticated to more and more complicated,
only from the less dense to the more dense. In all degrees of use,
from ornamental to highly organized, imagery appears to bisect the
timeline of Moravia's complete works. Metaphor and simile are all-

pervasive/invasive instruments that he uses to refract fictive reality or to describe that which in some way needs enrichment when conventional prose is insufficient. Imagery proposes an alternate mode of conceiving of what mimetic narrative pretends to be objective; it is part of an exquisite strategy to present what is "real" in a different way.

Thematically and stylistically the complete works form an integrated corpus which stands by itself as the macrocosm of the individual micro-units (novels, short stories, etc.). Taken as a whole picture, it is as though each novel or short story collection were but a chapter in the grand work; some are stronger, some weaker, but all are interdependent. Partly because of the extensive use of imagery, the *opera omnia* must also be examined as an entity unto itself. For in this respect, it is larger than the sum of its parts.

This study began with the goal of looking closely at Alberto Moravia as a stylist, to dispel the notion that the craft of writing was somehow not of interest to him. He is undeniably a stylist (and in some instances his flamboyant images trump the substance of his prose); but, in focusing on his use of imagery, interesting patterns arise that suggest certain attitudes, particularly relating to men and women. Moravia might be considered a stylistic-misogynist, as well as a stylistic master-craftsman; for his female characters usually emerge as negative portraits in his imagistic constructions, especially through his preoccupation with disparaging physical description.

Throughout the individual microcosmic works there is a shadow following certain categories of image-ized characters from work to work – a baggage they bring with them from novel to novel, short story to short story – an accumulation of images ascribed to all their counterparts. Even though their names change and they appear in different situations, the characters become freighted with the effects of imagery for the reader who has been bombarded with these constant allusions. A collective image eventually forms which the reader then grafts automatically onto the characters in the different categories. The resulting osmotic effect is that categorical images eventually apply to similar characters, no matter in what work they appear.

As Terry Eagleton writes, "A particular meaning in a poem will cause us retrospectively to revise what we have learnt already; a word or image which is repeated does not mean the same as it did the first time, by virtue of the very fact that it is a repetition. No event occurs twice, precisely because it has occurred once already" (116). Once the reader grasps the image that Moravia has created, subsequent images are colored by what the reader already knows.

But what does Moravia want to tell us at this level? What is the message conveyed by offering such a broad spectrum of images? Are there human values to be formulated by stepping back and examining the multiple layers of meaning? Deshler has called imagery "a 'handle' for perceiving organizational culture. That handle also may lead to understanding emotionally laden value meanings of cultural life within organizations. Metaphors contribute to what ethnographers call "thick" descriptions of a culture, descriptions that reflect subtle non-literal views of reality that yield potential explanations for overt behaviors and reactions to social structures" (22). Is Moravia's imagistic presentation of men and women a snapshot of western civilization, a "thick" description of our culture, or only the embodiment of the ideas of one author?

This bigger picture presents a marquetry of ideas and concepts that is lost when the individual works are considered singly and apart from their role in the larger scheme of things. For example, women are presented mostly in a negative light. And although men are also assigned negative images, Moravia pays more attention to the minds of men with his images, while, with rare exception, he does not consider the mental activities of a woman. It has been suggested that perhaps Moravia is trying to parody society's view of women with his use of imagery. A close look both at his pronouncements on women and at the vast majority his female characters suffices to disabuse oneself of that notion. It is more likely the case that the Moravian male character is an exercise in self-recognition, while the female seems to be a negative archytypal melange, perhaps on Moravia's part the very embodiment of Deshler's "non-literal views of reality."

Indeed it could be argued that in almost all cases, the images were created to underscore certain types, to make socially corrective points, all of which if true could very well accrue to the ultimate benefit of women (even if in a back-handed sort of way). By the same token, however, it can be argued that the imagery is a descriptive choice on Alberto Moravia's part, no matter what the purpose. He could have chosen to avoid such consistently and fiercely negative imagery. For in the works where it has no clear structural function, ostensibly imagery is there for descriptive embellishment, in which case, it could be answered, there are other ways to embellish. It is likely that Moravia never realized that his images were accumulating to such a revealing subtextual extent; it is also possible that he never really ascribed that much significance to the descriptive, "random" images that he was creating intertextually.

In Moravia's grand view, women are predominantly animals, food and deathly entities to be feared; woman is most often the object made, not the maker; she is not the sculptor, but the statue; not the player but the plaything. Men are machines, complicated by existential angst (and women); life is one big puzzle, war is . . . , etc. Barthes characterizes the rampant use of metaphor as it "rises up from the writer's myth-laden depths and unfolds beyond his area of control. It is the voice of hidden, secret flesh" (*Writing Degree Zero* 11). While it is not my intention nor within my field of expertise to psychoanalyze Moravia in this study, it should be clear even to the most naive reader that in his mimetic imagination half of the human race is tinged by an obdurate negativity. What does this mean to his female readers? Does he intend by implication for them to be as disenfranchised from full participation in critical discourse, political life, intellectual intercourse, as they are from equal and undemeaning participation as actors in his fiction? And if this is the case, does not our whole culture become impoverished? The answers seem clear.

Lakoff and Turner conclude that . . .

> to study metaphor is to be confronted with hidden aspects of one's own mind and one's own culture. (. . .) To do so is to discover that one has a world view, that one's imagination is constrained, and that metaphor plays an enormous role in shaping one's everyday understanding of everyday events. That is an important part of the power of poetic metaphor: it calls upon our deepest modes of everyday understanding and forces us to use them in new ways. (. . .) Recent discoveries about the nature of metaphor suggest that metaphor is anything but peripheral to the life of the mind. It is central to our understanding of our selves, our culture, and the world at large. Poetry, through metaphor, exercises our minds so that we can extend our normal powers of comprehension beyond the range of the metaphors we are brought up to see the world through. (214)

The "hidden aspects" of Moravia's mind become not so occult when one considers the implications of his imagery in general. Imagery is not "peripheral to the life of the mind"; it is pivotal in Moravia's world where the patterns of imagery create a whole undercurrent to his *opera omnia*. The primary aim of this study is to examine how style and content go hand-in-hand (how can we tell the dancer from the dance?). In doing that, however, what emerges as well is a picture which truly does clarify for us Moravia's worldview.

This architecture of imagery, Moravia's elegant narrative construction, reflects over sixty years of his thought, where style is never just the decorative handmaiden of content. Moravia wields his stylistic instruments with most intensity in his novels appearing *after* what is generally considered his "neo-realistic" period, but clearly, periodizing labels (neo-realistic, existential, etc.) mean little vis-à-vis such a wide-spread stylistic phenomenon. What emerges clearly is that Moravia cannot be dismissed as a writer lacking style, whatever the final effect. It is precisely his style, partly in the form of imagery, that functions as an overarching component of Moravia's *opera omnia*. Undeniably there is a non-accidental nature to the use of imagery; and there are broad implications in the arrangement of his metaphors and similes. Moravia's style is one very important key to understanding the thematics of his life's work. We need that illumination; for what we can see for ourselves, as Moravia writes in *L'uomo che guarda*, "è fuori metafora."

APPENDICES

APPENDIX A

LIST OF CATEGORIES

Categories in Descending Order of Recurrence:

I. *Imagery of Women*:

    a. women as animals
    b. women's body parts
    c. women as food
    d. women as dolls/marionettes/puppets
    e. women in miscellaneous categories
    f. women as objects/property
    g. women as goddesses/religious figures/decorative icons
    h. women as flowers/plants
    i. women as death
    j. women as machines
    k. women as masks
    l. women as conceptualizations

II. *Imagery of Men*:

    a. men as animals
    b. men's body parts
    c. men in miscellaneous categories
    d. men as puppets
    e. men as conceptualizations
    f. men as food
    g. men as machines
    h. men as masks
    i. men as plants/flowers
    j. man image-ized as a sexual partner

III. *Abstract Imagery*:

   a. abstract concepts
   b. thought
   c. ennui

IV. *War Imagery*:

   a. Nazis
   b. refugees (*sfollati*) and civilian population
   c. weapons
   d. effects of war
   e. Fascists
   f. Allies

V. *Concrete Imagery*

VI. *Imagery from the Natural/Physical World*:

   a. physical
   b. animals/insects/plants

VII. *Imagery of Architecture*

VIII. *Imagery of Machines*

IX. *Erotic Imagery*

X. *Imagery of the Human Body*

XI. *Food Imagery*

I. **Imagery of Women**

a. *Women as Animals*:

goat	chicken
marine animal	gorilla
sheep/lamb	bear
horse	frog
dog	cow/butcher-meat
rooster	caged beast
cat	snake
bird	lion

monkey
cow
calf
goose
snail
mouse
fox
pig
insect
June bug nearing a flame
elephant
seal
rhinoceros
wolf
whale

dinosaur
crab
leach
rabbit
swan
deer
butterfly
donkey
mule
chameleon
butterfly
panther
wild beast
dumb animal
general animals

b. *Women's Body Parts*:

woman's face = half-empty bag
                August moon
                medallion
                full moon
                large rose
                burning embers
                page boy
                Jack in a deck of cards
                horse
                wax
woman's head = heavy, pale acorn
bald woman = big, ugly egg
woman's profile = closed fist
woman's nose = negro/Polynesian fetish
                clapper (*batocchio*)
                carnival mask nose
woman's mouth = opening of a bank
                shapeless gash, laceration
                plunger
                wound
                oven
                red coral
                flower
woman's lips = rose
woman's tongue = snail
                pistil of a flower

woman's smile = sun on a dreary sky
woman's laugh = animal's call
woman's voice = strident cicada
woman's eyes = rays of a reflector
  balls
  slits
  pin points
  2 velvet stars
  2 stars in the summer night
  wet coal
  stars
  blue gem beneath agitated waters
woman's teeth = blooming almonds
woman's genitals = bar of soap
  wound
  buttonhole
  plunger
  cigar snipper
  pincushion
  plum
  shell
  smoke ring
  flower
  smooth palm of a hand
skeletal woman's sex organ = a warm bird's nest stuck in dry, cold
  tree branches in winter
female baby's genitals = thumbnail mark on wax
  vertical mouth lined up with the umbilical
  cord
  white mouth
woman's buttocks = twin spheres
woman's pants/tight at the inseam = wound
  fan
  sun's rays
woman's pubic hair = head of a goat
  seaweed around an anemone in clear water
woman's hair = priest's mitre
  pubic triangle
  serpent
woman's braid curling around her head = cord of a wicker basket
woman's breasts = two purses
  various fruits and vegetables
  flowers
  rubber squeeze-bulb of a claxon

extra large breasts = holds them like a baby
                     two innocent travellers forced to bounce
                     around by a skittish horse
          nipples = two dark coins
                    copper coins
woman's waist = wasp
woman's abdomen = an old suitcase
                  a silver tray
woman's legs = two clubs
               doors of treasure cave in "Sinbad the Sailor"
woman's thighs = jaws of a clamp
                 clamp
woman's sagging skin = sail without wind
woman's body = gymnasium
               old bedsheets
               pillow tied in two
               crucible
               white marble
               bottle: wide in the middle; thin at neck and base
with a girdle = tube/cylinder
woman's figure with luminescent curves = threads of nylon
woman takes care of her body = soldier with his gun
woman's fat = contrabass in its case
              amphora
              barrel

c. *Women as Food*:

fruit	roast chicken
watermelon	egg
apple	eggs/omelet
cherry	bread
plum	reheated soup
oranges	chestnut
pear	wine
medlar	milk
peach	anise
onion	liqueur
Savoy cabbage	*la pasta sfusa*
pumpkin	sack of flour or sugar
meat	bar or buffet
steak	banquet
bone	generic food or drink

d. *Women as Dolls/Marionettes/Puppets*:

marionette	Christmas tree ornament
puppet	mannequin
doll	baby

e. *Women in Miscellaneous Categories*:

dog's master (man as dog)
goal-tender (man as soccer player)
burnt-out candle
earth
terrain
sleepwalker
streetwalker
bellows
symbolic sign
teacher
actress
hunter
prisoner
devourer
witch
recipe
drug
baby
scarecrow
timeless, spaceless creature
Jack of spades
gendarme
moon's two sides
sibyl
jewel
beautiful boat
quiet waters
locks (men are keys)
broken vase
saint
precious metal
martyr
victim
self-torturer

spinning top
black woman = photographic negative image
fighting women = fish wives
women's mannerisms = odor of bread ovens
woman's emptiness = hanging clothes
female child = prostitute
sex-starved woman = drug addict
                        nicotine addict
hiding woman = a little girl in love
apathetic woman = calloused hand
flighty woman's life = ashtray full of half-smoked butts
woman performing oral sex = baby being fed
woman's oppressive conversation = sultry weather (*afa*)
woman's presence = like an urgent message
woman's impressionable sensitivity = an X-ray

f. *Women as Objects/Property*:

object of property	rental property
bait for a male's trap	gold
commercial product	

g. *Women as Goddesses/Religious Figures/Decorative Icons*:

statue	sarcophagus sculpture
ancient Roman statue	priestess
made of marble	high priestess
angel figure	oracle
angel of the Annunciation	sibyl
goddess	nautical figurehead
artist's model	decorative monsters
madonna	ancient frescoes
primitive madonna	sphynx
Modigliani painting	amphora
Etruscan statue	Venus

h. *Women as Flowers/Plants*:

bouquet of wildflowers
rosebud
dead flowers
lightening-struck tree (vis-à-vis man as a fallen tree)
reed
fruit tree

unwatered plant
unopened flower bud
blooming flowers
flower as a symbol of the inexorability of nature
dried flower
open rose
squashed geranium
upside-down rose
low class grass
plant left to die
withered flower
a hot-house flower which dies when taken outdoors
non-clinging vine

i. *Women as Death*:

decapitated head   death
skeleton   angel of death
mummy

j. *Women as Machines*:

machine   automaton
car   robot

k. *Women as Masks*:

silk mask
gesso mask
painted face mask
woman associated with primitive African masks
threatening mask of make-up
death mask
make-up
carnival mask
overly made-up mask
wooden mask
fixed mask
inhuman, cruel mask

l. *Women as Conceptualizations*:

bored woman = falls like a feather in a stairwell
women's lives = a rickety box having fallen out of a truck and
    broken open with contents scattered everywhere

suffering woman = Jesus in Gethsemane the night before Judas
  came to get him
two women alone without a man to protect them = two blind per-
  sons who walk without seeing or understanding where they are

II. Imagery of Men

a. *Men as Animals*:

rooster

sick, old rooster when it opens its eyes
  wide and is listless and refuses to eat

chicken

ostrich

dog

bird

featherless, ugly bird

unhealthy bird

cat

wolffish

shark

snail

bull

bear

leopard

snake

eel

rabbit

tiger

monkey

gorilla

cricket

pig

sheep

goat

peacock

worm

beef cattle

lizard

mouse

spider

insect

ram

goat

lamb

ox

donkey

seal

flea

elephant

boar

turkey

marine animal

horse

calf

hyena

rhinoceros

crab

squirrel

frog

turtle

bestia

b. *Men's Body Parts*:

man's mouth = knife cut
                cut
                round hole with concentric wrinkles like razor cuts
                broken purse

slot in a child's savings bank
boat with upturned ends
man's smile = half-moon
crescent moon
man's frown = cloud in front of moon
man's nose = hook
beak
drill
pitcher handle
butter
clapper (*batocchio*)
butcher's bloody meat hook
tip of man's nose = a *gnocco*
spout of a clay cooking pot (*pignatta*)
man's face = rock
two pieces of blue glass in a bunch of rags
icebag
melting wax
samurai
orange skin
fist
a pale moon
egg; shirt collar is egg cup
lit up like a lantern
fallen like a meteor
a fearful, inexplicable object that lightening reveals for
an instant
shadow and light on a statue
pock-marked face = fallen peach or apple, spotted and cut, rotten
inside
man's head = trunk (*baule*)
owl
insect
silkworm
clay pot (*pignatta*)
ivory
man's forehead = forehead of a bird
man's blonde hair = twigs of a wicker basket
man's eyes = tv screen
turquoise
two glass vortices
pig eyes
two calm stars

mask
two pieces of coal under the ashes
almonds
two pieces of the sea
fish eyes
two black olives
man's eyes gazing on money = kite bird flying over a chicken
man's ears = raised like an animal's
man's voice = distant like a record on a grammophone slowing down
        ogre
man's penis = clapper
        bell
man's impotent penis = newborn's red, wrinkled face
man's belly = pear
man's arm = iron cable
man's legs = ostrich legs
man's pumping arms = handles of a pair of bellows
man's baldness = knee
man's body = Pompeiian cast (*calco*)
        2 large balls, one atop the other
thin man = nail
shrivelled man = dry chestnut
man wasted away = candle

c. *Men in Miscellaneous Categories*:

Man = spectator
        bad, provincial actor
        pirate
        prodigal son
        hunter (woman = prey)
        steam shovel
        stuffed bag
        jewel
        electric wire
        wandering Jew
        saint
        butcher
        mountain lake
        sleepwalker
        puppeteer (to woman's being a puppet)
        double exposure
        meteor
        fairy tale midget

d. *Men as Puppets*:

puppet
inanimate statue
straw-man
mannequin
automaton

e. *Men as Conceptualizations*:

man's confused brain = explosion in a china shop
man's impulse to confide in strangers suddenly stops = a boat
    whose keel has met an obstacle
man's flash of illumination = flame of a short circuit
man's woman exhibits knowledge he never knew she had = like
    finding other human footprints on a deserted island
man finally understands = the tip of the iceberg of exact knowledge
    that could sink a ship
man clears up a misunderstanding = characters in a classic comedy
    before the happy ending
man's exploding hypothesis = colorful soap bubbles
man takes stock of a situation = contemplating the broken pieces of
    a precious object
man clings to woman = drowning man to the mast of a sinking ship
man = poetic appendix of woman's vulgar personality
man's whole being = digital numbers
man assumes fetal position = clothes in an automatic washing
    machine as seen through the porthole
man wants to conform = large army
man = a dead star with woman as a mirror of his apathy
man sees a woman nude; his thoughts fly away = a flock of
    sparrows leaving a tree when a gun is shot
man dying of fright = melting like a candle, each day more and
    more
very organized man = a travel agency
man's exhilaration = a stormy sea
man's life = a stormy sea
diffident man = prey to seduction like an easy woman who feels her
    breast and hips being pinched
abandoned man = a ship in a storm
man learns to reason = a plant that sends out branches wherever
    there is sunshine

f. *Men as Food*:

lemon
red apples
chestnut
tripe
salame
octopus
valves of a shell
neither meat nor fish
bread
butterball
sugar
champagne

g. *Men as Machines*:

tv screen
digital machine
flour mill
hi-fi system
steam shovel
machine
robot

h. *Men as Masks*:

carneval mask
Pompeiian satyr
mask of the *Bocca della Verità* in Rome
mask

i. *Men as Plants and Flowers*:

tree
fresh flowers
wildflower
vineyard

j. *Men Image-ized as a Sexual Partner*:

man's foreplay = priest at the altar
man's pre-lovemaking = man looking at the door
man atop woman = hot meat matress
male voyeur = spectator at a sporting event
                    hunter hiding

supine man = St. Sebastian tied to a pole
seducer = a surgeon
persistent seducer = a lumberjack who after each blow of the
   hatchet observes the tree to see if it is about to fall

III. Abstract Imagery

a. *Abstract Concepts*:

coldness = tomb
reality = Chinese box
concrete reality = found like an artist finds his inspiration in
   happier times
words create an atmosphere = like an octopus in its ink
life = whore
        uncomfortable bed
        whirlwind
        rickety as a box fallen out of a truck, broken open with
           its contents strewn everywhere
the world = rebus
actions merely suggesting existence = plaster casts (*calci*) at
   Pompeii
a thread = recollection (vis-à-vis hole of a needle = memory)
envy = rubber ball
Hiroshima's effect of leaving the print of the human body on the
   wall = existence of characters in a novel through writing and
   the imagination
memories = flotsam and jetsom
false guilt = taking off a bandage and finding the wound healed
hate = monster emerging from the sea
life of boredom = rides at a carneval
a "force" = puppydog
desperation = wild beast
desperation = cross section of a complicated airplane engine in a
   travel agent's window
despair mixed with hope = two rivers coming together
worry = termite
alienation = sidereal spaces
unhappy feeling = taking a step thinking there is a stair and instead
   stepping on flatness and losing one's balance
bitter expression = cloud on the land
two lives = rivers separating then reuniting
love = flowering plant with roots in fertilizer

creative energy = serpent
truth reveals itself = venus fly trap
imagination = wild horse
everything dear disappears = trees in a cyclone that fall to earth
spirits = pickled vegetables
genius = caged beast (cage = *documenti umani*)
seemingly random actions = not like flowers in a field or stones on
    a pebbly bank, but aligned like disciplined soldiers
conversation without seeing face and body = reading a libretto
    without music or a scenography without the image on the screen
choices = Siamese twins with a plus and a minus side
lying on divan = lying on doctor's examining table
feeling silly = cripple trying to dance
nervous convulsion = epileptic fit
discovery = blind person from birth who can suddenly see
anger explodes = wound-up spring
pain = wound-up spring
      thorn
painful image = branding iron
science = a house of cards
presage of war = the beginning of a storm when leaves on trees all
    turn in one direction, and sheep gather together and wind
    blows close to the ground
sleep clouds one's head = wine on an empty stomach
good sleep = homemade bread
bad sleep = black tar
long over-due sleep = winding up a wound-down watch
eating and drinking for rurals = having a car and apartment in the
    Parioli for Romans
youth = strength of a tree, quiet under the sun
rural pride in eggs and lard = Roman women's pride in evening wear
religion for the religious = the air that one breathes without taking
    notice
fragile human perfection = a house of cards
danger = a rare and delectable sauce
returning to one's roots = uprooted plants replanted in native
    territory
abandoning native land = light rags tossed about by life
glances of a nasty man stick to a woman's back = two leeches
people appear in a scene = the countryside illuminated by the
    lightening of a storm
secret shame = worms in a decomposing body
absent minded stare = triple vision through defective vision

irritation over a misunderstanding = gasps of a wounded animal
  that will not die
unsuccessful search for a lost object = catching an agile, small animal,
  a mouse or a butterfly
unpleasant situation = an ugly, dilapidated house that must be
  patched up without the possibility of rebuilding

b. *Thought*:

quick thought then blankness of mind = sudden whirlwind then
  nothing
quickly formulated thought = child's jigsaw puzzle
depth of thought = fog
good idea = bubble rising to the surface
idea = toy spinning top
    mask
    cold knife blade
thoughts = nuts in an empty bag
thought = ball bouncing on a wall
empty thoughts = ant hill
absence of cognizance = wooden planks, boards
associations of thought = horseflies
mental voice = fish outside the whorl of a marine vortex
incipient thought = bird on sill
internal voice = a soldier taking back a deserter
rush of thoughts = birds in cage

c. *Ennui*:

ennui = too-short blanket
    interruption of electricity
    sickness of objects
    unpleasant train companion
    fog
    dark cloud
mental inertia = lead

IV. **War Imagery**

a. *Nazis*:

savage beast
poisonous snake
tiger

furious wolf
entrapped wild animal which still threatens and bares its teeth
escaping rabbits
Nazi soldier with a quirk = certain trees which grow against a wall
    and have all their branches only on the side opposite the wall
Nazi lieutenant in uniform = flat as a sheet of paper
                         dog
Nazi soldier's scarred face = peach or apple fallen from a tree,
    covered with spots and cuts, inside half-rotten
Nazi soldier's pale face = paper
                         dog
                      beaten dog
Nazi soldier's jaw = mastiff
          eyes = beast
Nazi soldier answering questions about war = puffed up with self-
importance like a balloon
Nazi soldier = a savage beast which purrs and then bares its teeth
jumpy Nazi soldier = frog at the side of a swamp
Nazi soldiers escape = hares
Nazis fight = eating an artichoke leaf by leaf – first annihilate the
    civilians in the valley then those in the mountains
Swastika = a running, four-legged ugly insect
Hitler's mustache = toothbrush
              eyes = rotten fish

b.   *Refugees (sfollati) and Civilian Population*:

    starving civilians, picking cicory = souls in Purgatory
    civilians terrified of bombings = rabbits in their warrens
    a plundered family screams = "come da un Purgatorio"
    sfollati being strafed = sparrows being tracked by a hunter
    sfollati resting in sunshine = shivering lizards
    sfollati = uprooted plants away from homeland
            light tattered rags
    war dead = heaps of dirty clothes
    living women repeatedly raped in war = dead bodies
    women refugees on a mountain top = birds roosting above a flood
    family of *sfollati* before retiring = chickens in a hen house agitated
        before going to sleep
    frightened children vis-à-vis their mother = puppies jumping at
        their mother
    sfollati defecate = as animals do
    refugees caught in a German dragnet = little fish in a big net
    refugees leave home = nude and rustic like gypsies

cautious refugee gives bread to Nazis = like one treats untrustworthy
   wild animals
war-affected, uneducated men = animals
war-affected sharecroppers = animals
war-affected farmers = animals
scurrying civilians = mice when cat arrives
civilians crowded into trams = animals going to the butcher
civilian life during winter of 1944 = animals
anti-Fascist crowd = floodwaters
Italians in favor of German soldiers = flies or roaches

c. *Weapons*:

airplane = black insect
      fly
strafing airplane = a hunter on a lark with his dog in the brush
two women as airplane's prey = two sparrows
English airplane = pins of silver filigree made in Venice
English bombs = ripe fruit falling from a shaken tree
red flames from a wounded plane = scarf in the breeze of blue sky
cannon = fist pounding on a drum
cannon tracings in sky = wounds
                  razor slits in sky with dripping blood
cannon following target = admonishing finger
abandoned cannon in a field = ugly animal wounded and left
knives = displayed like a fan
flack = cloudy efflorescence
shelling hits a house = children's house of cards
modern battle = a housewife with a spray can of insecticide killing
    flies without dirtying her hands

d. *Effects of War*:

sky during Allied bombing = skin of a drum
strafing noise = the pounding of a sewing machine
war-torn town with *sfollati,* civilians, soldiers = a county fair
war-torn houses' black windows = the eyes of the blind
war = dying, horrible animal ("può sempre dare qualche zampata")

e. *Fascists*:

Fascist = devils from hell
cowardly Fascists = rats when the cat arrives
footsoldiers = animals
Fascist flag = black mourning cloth
Fascism/Nazism = a crumbling prison house of lies and fear

f. *Allies*:

Allies = local saints who perform miracles, bring rain and good
weather
American soldier's face = a closed fist
Russian soldier's eyes = two pieces of the deepest blue sea
Mongol prisoners of war = two big monkeys
allied motorcyclists of a column of walking soldiers = sheepdogs
who busy themselves around a slow, lazy flock of sheep

V. Concrete Imagery

sleepwalker = actor
small pieces of farmland = small handkerchiefs
goat droppings = bayberries
twisting road = serpent
rough draft for a novel = skeleton
bureaucrats = lost souls in torment
flagstones = round loaves of bread
hot Rome = load of dirty laundry
men dressed in overalls = procession of angels
fire = red flower
butcher block = altar to its butcher
upper class in a bus = Jordan almonds (*confetti*) in silk candy box
(*bomboniera*)
body having undergone plastic surgery = football
arguing people = *tamburello* players
pulled up dress = theatre curtain
painter's empty canvas = boredom
wet asphalt = snake skin
asphalt = the back of an animal hot from blood and life
cracks in asphalt = cracked skin
radios playing in unison = roosters crowing at dawn
sports car with chrome grate = a tiger
trite phrases = bats
pensione = wild beast
Octopus carneval ride (*ottovolante*) = paralyzed, pot-bellied insects
police station = beehive
tight dress = spiderweb
clothing for woman = blue sky for prisoner
glance = fly
crest of nobility = insect

man perusing a book = bird flying over land looking to alight
street = serpent
     woman's open legs
street sign = burnt phantoms
four-way street corner = an empty theatrical scene
mountain path = serpent warmed by the first warmth of spring
dancing = toy spinning top
words = sheep inexorably jumping over a cliff
baby's eyes = seed sprouting
eye-lids = sea urchins
red light = winking eye
trite phrases = flies on flypaper
scippo artist = hunter
     victim = fat quail
lawyers on their prey = sharp-toothed sharks on a soft whale
lawyers' accusations = bricks of a demolished building
couple = actors
bracing shower = pins being shot at the cranium
supine couple = twin sepulchres
children = kite birds
Polaroid photo emerging from camera = tongue sticking out
Africans = photographic negative images
destroyed piano's keys = animal's jaw with teeth
violin music = entwining tropical plant
     serpent in love
coal shop = mouth of an oven
flare = flower
money = a person's best and only friend
wad of money clutched by a greedy person = talons of a falcon or
    kite bird
heaving floor = the deck of a ship
candle smoke = black snakes
votive light = hope of returning home

VI. Imagery of the Natural/Physical World

a. *Physical*:

    moon = copper pot lid
        ornament
    moon's phases = curved hem
           sickle
           silver disk

star in the sky = diamond on a woman's forehead
twinkling stars = golden eyes that look and know everything about us
sun = jewel
    gold
first ray of sun = golden arrow
sunlight = golden eyes
winter sun = a convalescent wrapped in cotton
intense sunlight = certain physical pains so strong and intolerable
    worsening with each passing minute
filtering light = water into a sinking ship
overused light = the material of an old dress
spreading shadow = a photographic plate burned by the sun
roiling clouds = intestines in distress
clouds = grey cotton
storm clouds over the sea = as over a boiling pot
sky = fresh paint
    piece of crystal
    drum
    open fan of clouds, handle toward the sea and fan's struts
      (clouds) spoking through the sky
rain = humid and smoky veil
wind = far-away harp
heavy, grey air on a street = steam arising from very dirty laundry
ocean's surface = lead scratched with a knife
dark waves = back/rump of an amphibious animal
sea = satin
water = crystal
wake of water = lace on the silk of the sea
glacier = an animal
forest = man's beard
lush land after winter = bald woman
countryside = fresh lettuce
terraced earth = immense staircase
leaves = yellow hands
    gold
ivy = flounces on a dress
branches of the holm-oak = arms
prickly pear = little swollen faces
sprouting grain = velvet
trees = twisted like snakes
fruit trees in bloom = white and pink clouds
unleafed branches of an oak tree = witches' tresses
defoliated natural spot = a bald woman

benevolent countryside = an old, wise, good and forgiving mother
trees' nude branches = unknotted serpents awakening from dormancy
trees in an expanse of cement = hairs of an armpit
large rock = *panettone*
cliffs = smooth, black sugar loaves
barren rock = sugar loaves
        grey, elephant skin
natural world = war where everything seems normal but underneath people are scared and escape when they can

b. *Animals/Insects/Plants*:

cat follows master = like a puppy
goat skin attached to meat = poorly glued sheet of paper
bloated goat, to-be-butchered = wineskin
goat skin is removed = glove
goat skin tossed aside = used item of clothing
goat's intestines = skein
goat's blood draining = fountain
roaches scattering = frenetic dance
roach powder = atomic bomb
chimpanzee = person
chimpanzee's nose = *gnocco*
hippopotamus = *cotica*
monkey's rump = eggplant
lizard = human potential

VII. **Imagery of Architecture**

apartment = dogpound
balconies of an apartment building = soap holders
room = a small cave
bedroom = womb
corridor = intestines
Colosseum = a skull
cupola of St. Peter's = atomic mushroom cloud
narrator's mother's study = religious temple
Latin-American dictator's villa = house in Ithaca
        dictator's wife = Penelope
sanatorium = womb
Roman ruin = *panettone*
house = cave
        mirror

house in a storm = a crazed toy top
house's illuminated windows = walls of a sunlit aquarium
newsstand = theatre
terrace = stage

VIII. **Imagery of Machines**

car's motor = beehive
cars = beetles
    motionless flock of sheep
    life
    whale washed up by a flood
randomly parked cars = dominoes
car moving through traffic = cetacean
car and bus front-end = snout of a dog
tram = thresher
    merry-go-round
motorscooter = horse
        ass
        mule
        dead insect
motor's sound = bees
helicopter = dragonfly

IX. **Erotic Imagery**

eroticism = volcano
lovemaking = plunger
orgasm = epileptic fit
incest = dead larva in a dried up cocoon
sexual indifference = gift from savage to explorer
observing nudity = child looking through a keyhole
woman's blowing skirts = a billowing theatrical curtain

X. **Imagery of the Human Body**
(not related to specific men and women)

nose wart = a *cece* bean
muscles = iron
blue eyes = hard stone
teeth = ivory
eyes = ice chest

XI. Images of Food

champagne = orgasm
Savoy cabbage = baby's head
onions = sword

APPENDIX B

Moravia's Prose Works

Gli indifferenti, Milano: Alpes, 1929
La bella vita, Lanciano: Carabba, 1935
Le ambizioni sbagliate, Milano: Mondadori, 1935
L'imbroglio, Milano: Mondadori, 1937
Cosma e i briganti, Oggi, 1940; Sellerio, 1980
I sogni del pigro, Milano: Bompiani, 1940
La mascherata, Milano: Bompiani, 1941
La cetonia, Roma: Documento, 1943
L'amante infelice, Milano: Bompiani, 1943
Agostino, Roma: Documento, 1943
L'epidemia, Roma: Documento, 1944
Due cortigiane, Roma: Acquario, 1945
La romana, Milano: Bompiani, 1947
La disubbidienza, Milano: Bompiani, 1948
L'amore coniugale, Milano: Bompiani, 1949
Il conformista, Milano: Bompiani, 1951
I racconti di Moravia, Milano: Bompiani, 1952
Romanzi brevi: La mascherata, Agostino, La disubbidienza, L'amore coniugale, Milano: Bompiani, 1953
Racconti romani, Milano: Bompiani, 1954
Il disprezzo, Milano: Bompiani, 1954
Racconti surrealistici e satirici: L'epidemia, I sogni del pigro, Milano: Bompiani, 1956
La ciociara, Milano: Bompiani, 1957
Teatro: La mascherata, Beatrice Cenci, Milano: Bompiani, 1958
Nuovi racconti romani, Milano: Bompiani, 1959
La noia, Milano: Bompiani, 1960
L'automa, Milano: Bompiani, 1962
La cortigiana stanca, Milano: Bompiani, 1965

L'attenzione, Milano: Bompiani, 1965
Il mondo è quello che è, L'intervista, Milano: Bompiani, 1966
Una cosa è una cosa, Milano: Bompiani, 1967
Moravia Classici: Le ambizioni sbagliate, Gli indifferenti, Milano: Bompiani, 1967
Il dio Kurt, Milano: Bompiani, 1968
La vita è gioco, Milano: Bompiani, 1969
Il paradiso, Milano: Bompiani, 1970
Io e lui, Milano: Bompiani, 1971
Un'altra vita, Milano: Bompiani, 1973
Boh!, Milano: Bompiani, 1976
La vita interiore, Milano: Bompiani, 1978
Storie e preistorie, Milano: Bompiani, 1982
1934, Milano: Bompiani, 1982
La cosa, Milano: Bompiani, 1983
L'uomo che guarda, Milano: Bompiani, 1985
Il viaggio a Roma, Milano: Bompiani, 1988
La villa del venerdì, Milano: Bompiani, 1990
La donna leopardo, 1991

WORKS CITED

Aristotle. Poetics. *The Works of Aristotle.* Trans. Ingram Bywater. Oxford: Claren-
don P, 1924.
Barthes, Roland. *Le bruissement de la langue.* Paris: Editions du Seuil, 1984.
———. *S/Z* Trans. Richard Miller. New York: Farrar, Straus and Giroux, 1974.
———. *Writing Degree Zero.* Trans. Annette Lavers and Colin Smith. Boston: Bea-
con Press, 1967.
Biasin, Gian Paolo. "Lucia secondo Moravia." *Verri.* ns 5. 11 (1975), 56-69.
Black, Max. "Metaphor." *Proceedings of the Aristotelian Society* (1954-55). ns LV.
London: Harrison, 1955.
———. *Models and Metaphors.* Ithaca: Cornell UP, 1962.
Brooke-Rose, Christine. *A Grammar of Metaphor.* London: Secker and Warburg, 1958.
Burke, Kenneth. *A Grammar of Motives.* New York: Prentice, 1945.
Caruso, Liliana and Bibi Tomasi. *I padri della fallocultura.* Milano: SugarCo, 1974.
Cottrell, Jane. *Alberto Moravia.* New York: Ungar, 1974.
Crocenzi, Lilia. *La donna nella narrativa di A. Moravia.* Cremona: Gianni Mangia-
rotti, 1966.
del Buono, Oreste. *Moravia.* Milano: Feltrinelli, 1962.
Deshler, David. "Metaphors and Values in Higher Education." *Academe.* Novem-
ber-December 1985, 22-28.
Donoghue, Denis. "The Strange Case of Paul de Man." *New York Review.* June 29,
1989, 32-37.
Eagleton, Terry. *Literary Theory: An Introduction.* Minneapolis: University of Min-
nesota Press, 1983.
Eco, Umberto. *Postscript to the Name of the Rose.* New York: Harcourt, 1984.
Fernandez, Dominique. *Il romanzo italiano e la crisi della coscienza moderna.* Mi-
lano: Lerici, 1960.
Gilligan, Carol. *In a Different Voice.* Cambridge: Harvard UP, 1982.
Goleman, Daniel. "Research Probes What the Mind Senses Unaware." *New York
Times.* August 13, 1990.
Goodman, Nelson. *Languages of Art.* Indianapolis: Bobbs-Merrill, 1968.
Haynes, Felicity. "Metaphor as Interactive." *Educational Theory* 25. 3 (1975), 273.
Heiney, Donald. *Three Italian Novelists: Moravia, Pavese, Vittorini.* Ann Arbor:
University of Michigan P, 1968.
Kibler, Louis. "Imagery as Expression: Moravia's *Gli indifferenti.*" *Italica.* XLIX. 3
(1972), 315-334.
Kozma, Janice M. "Metaphor in Pratolini's Novels: *Il quartiere* and *Cronache di
poveri amanti.*" *Romance Notes.* 20.3 (1980) 1-6.
———. "Functions of Metaphor in Pratolini's *Cronache di poveri amanti*: Maciste
and the Signora." *Italian Culture.* 3 (1981) 87-102.

Kozma, Janice M. "Pratolini's *Il quartiere*: The Metaphor." *Kentucky Romance Quarterly*. 29.1 (1982) 37-45.

———. "Omen and Image: Presage and Sacrifice in Moravia's *La ciociara*." *Italica*. 61.3 (1984), 207-19.

Krajic, Kevin. "Sound Too Good To Be True?" *Newsweek*. July 30, 1990. 61.

Kristeva, Julia. *The Kristeva Reader*. Ed. Toril Moi. New York: Columbia UP, 1986.

———. *Desire in Language*. Ed. Leon Roudiez. Trans. Thomas Gora, Alice Jardine, Leon Roudiez. New York: Columbia UP, 1980.

Lacan, Jacques. *Ecrits/A Selection*. New York: Norton, 1977.

Lakoff, George and Mark Johnson, *Metaphors We Live By*. Chicago: University of Chicago P, 1980.

Lakoff, George and Mark Turner, *More than Cool Reason: A Field Guide to Poetic Metaphor*. Chicago: University of Chicago Press, 1989.

McGrath, Peter. "The Lessons of Munich." *Newsweek*. October 3, 1988.

Miller, George A. "Images and Models, Similes and Metaphors." in *Metaphor and Thought*. Ed. Andrew Ortony. New York: Cambridge UP, 1979.

Miller, Mark Crispin. "Hollywood: The AD." *Atlantic Monthly*. April, 1990. 41-68.

Minore, Renato. "Giovani timidi e signore strabiche." *Il Messaggero*. June 19, 1990.

Moravia, Alberto. *Un'altra vita*. Milano: Bompiani, 1973.

———. *L'attenzione*. Milano: Bompiani, 1965.

———. *Boh!* Milano: Bompiani, 1976.

———. *La ciociara*. Milano: Bompiani, 1965.

———. *Il conformista*. Milano: Bompiani, 1951.

———. *La cosa*. Milano: Bompiani, 1983.

———. "Differenza tra artista e intellettuale." *Il Corriere della Sera*. 5 November, 1972: 8.

———. *La donna leopardo*. Milano: Bompiani, 1991.

———. *Intervista sullo scrittore scomodo*. With Nello Aiello. Roma: Laterza, 1978.

———. *Io e lui*. Milano: Bompiani, 1971.

———. *La noia*. Milano: Bompiani, 1960.

———. *Nuovi racconti romani*. Milano: Bompiani, 1959.

———. *Il paradiso*. Milano: Bompiani, 1970.

———. *Racconti romani*. Milano: Bompiani, 1954.

———. *La romana*. Milano: Bompiani, 1965.

———. "Tuttolibri." *La Stampa*. With Mirella Serri. XII. 536. 17 January 1987: 4.

———. *L'uomo che guarda*. Milano: Bompiani, 1985.

———. *L'uomo come fine e altri saggi*. Opere complete 15. I Edizione. Milano: Bompiani, 1976.

———. *La vita è gioco*. Milano: Bompiani, 1969.

———. *La vita interiore*. Milano: Bompiani, 1978.

———. *1934*. Milano: Bompiani, 1985.

Moravia, Alberto and Alain Elkann. *Vita di Moravia*. Milano: Bompiani, 1990.

Murray, J. Middleton. "Metaphor." *Countries of the Mind*. Second Series. London: 1931.

Pratolini, Vasco. *Il quartiere*. Milano: Mondadori, 1964.

Quaranta, Bruno. "Voltolini: La metropoli è un'invenzione." *La Stampa. Tutto libri*. 20 January 1990: 2.

Radcliff-Umstead, Douglas. "Moravia's Indifferent Puppets." *Symposium*. XXIV. 1. Spring 1970, 44-54.

Ragusa, Olga. "Voyeurism and Storytelling." *The Southern Review*. 4 January 1968, 141.

Richards, I. A. *The Philosophy of Rhetoric*. Oxford UP, 1936. Rpt. in *Philosophical Perspectives on Metaphor*. Ed. Mark Johnson. Minneapolis: University of Minnesota P, 1981, 48-62.

Ricoeur, Paul. *La métaphore vive*. Paris: Editions du Seuil, 1975.
―――. *The Rule of Metaphor*. Trans. Robert Czerny. Toronto: University of Toron-
  to Press, 1977.
Romani, Cinzia. "Io e le donne." *La Stampa. Tutto libri*. 2 June, 1990.
Romano, Carlin. "Mighty like a Metaphor." *Voice Literary Supplement*. December
  1981, 9.
Strappini, Lucia. *Le cose e le figure negli Indifferenti di Moravia*. Roma: Bulzoni,
  1978.
Suleiman, Susan Rubin (ed.), *The Female Body in Western Culture*. Cambridge:
  Harvard UP, 1986.
Swanson, Don R. "Afterthoughts." *On Metaphor*. Ed. Sheldon Sacks. University of
  Chicago Press, 1978.
Tait, Foster. Foreword. *The Myth of Metaphor*. By Collin Murray Turbayne. Colum-
  bia: South Carolina UP, 1971.
Turbayne, Colin Murray. *The Myth of Metaphor*. Columbia: South Carolina UP,
  1971.
Verga, Giovanni. *Tutte le novelle*. Milano: Mondadori, 1970.
Vittorini, Elio. *Erica e i suoi fratelli*. Milano: Bompiani, 1956.
Wellek, René and Austin Warren. *Theory of Literature*. Harcourt, 1956.
Wood, Sharon. *Woman as Object*. London: Pluto Press, 1990.

SELECTED BIBLIOGRAPHY

Baldini Mezzalana, Bruna. *Alberto Moravia e l'alienazione.* Milano: Ceschina, 1971.

Berggren, Douglas. "The Use and Abuse of Metaphor." *The Review of Metaphysics* 16, 2 (1962): 237-258; 3 (1963): 450-472.

Castelli, Eugenio. *Tres narradores italianos: Alberto Moravia, Carlo Cassola, Giuseppe Dessi.* Argentina: Colmegna, 1978.

Dego, Giuliano. *Moravia.* NY: Barnes and Noble, 1967.

de Lauretis, Teresa. *Alice Doesn't: Feminism, Semiotics, Cinema.* Bloomington: Indiana UP, 1984.

de Man, Paul. "The Epistemology of Metaphor." *Critical Inquiry* 5, 1 (1978) 13-30.

De Michelis, Eurialo. *Introduzione a Moravia.* Firenze: La nuova Italia, 1954.

Groppali, Enrico. *L'ossessione e il fantasma.* Venezia: Marsilio, 1979.

Limentani, Alberto. *Alberto Moravia tra esistenza e realtà.* Venezia: Neri Pozza, 1962.

Mascia Galateria, Marinella. *Come leggere Gli indifferenti di Alberto Moravia.* Milano: Mursia, 1975.

Miall, David S. (ed.). *Metaphor: Problems and Perspectives.* Sussex: Harvester Press, 1982.

Pacifici, Sergio. *The Modern Italian Novel from Pea to Moravia.* Carbondale: Southern Illinois UP, 1979.

Piccioni, Leone. *La narrativa italiana tra romanzo e racconti.* Milano: Mondadori, 1959.

Pullini, Giorgio. *Il romanzo italiano del dopoguerra.* Milano: Schwarz, 1961.

Ravaioli, Carla. *La mutazione femminile.* Milano: 1975.

Rebay, Luciano. *Alberto Moravia.* New York: 1970.

Sanguinetti, Edoardo. *Alberto Moravia.* Milano: Mursia, 1962.

Saviane, Sergio. *Moravia desnudo.* Milano: SugarCo, 1976.

Shibles, Warren. *Metaphor: An Annotated Bibliography and History.* Whitewater, Wisconsin: The Language Press, 1971.

Siciliano, Enzo. *Alberto Moravia.* Milano: Bompiani, 1982.

Tessari, Roberto. *Alberto Moravia.* Firenze: Le Monnier, 1977.

Wheelwright, Philip. *Metaphor and Reality.* Bloomington: Indiana University Press, 1962.

INDEX

NORTH CAROLINA STUDIES IN THE ROMANCE LANGUAGES AND LITERATURES

I.S.B.N. Prefix 0-8078-

Recent Titles

When ordering please cite the *ISBN Prefix* plus the last four digits for each title.

Send orders to: University of North Carolina Press
P.O. Box 2288
CB# 6215
Chapel Hill, NC 27515-2288
U.S.A.

NORTH CAROLINA STUDIES IN THE ROMANCE LANGUAGES AND LITERATURES

I.S.B.N. Prefix 0-8078-

Recent Titles

THE BROKEN ANGEL: MYTH AND METHOD IN VALÉRY, by Ursula Franklin. 1984. (No. 222). *-9226-2.*

READING VOLTAIRE'S CONTES: A SEMIOTICS OF PHILOSOPHICAL NARRATION, by Carol Sherman. 1985. (No. 223). *-9227-0.*

THE STATUS OF THE READING SUBJECT IN THE "LIBRO DE BUEN AMOR", by Marina Scordilis Brownlee. 1985. (No. 224). *-9228-9.*

MARTORELL'S TIRANT LO BLANCH: A PROGRAM FOR MILITARY AND SOCIAL REFORM IN FIFTEENTH-CENTURY CHRISTENDOM, by Edward T. Aylward. 1985. (No. 225). *-9229- 7.*

NOVEL LIVES: THE FICTIONAL AUTOBIOGRAPHIES OF GUILLERMO CABRERA INFANTE AND MARIO VARGAS LLOSA, by Rosemary Geisdorfer Feal. 1986. (No. 226). *-9230-0.*

SOCIAL REALISM IN THE ARGENTINE NARRATIVE, by David William Foster. 1986. (No. 227). *-9231-9.*

HALF-TOLD TALES: DILEMMAS OF MEANING IN THREE FRENCH NOVELS, by Philip Stewart. 1987. (No. 228). *-9232-7.*

POLITIQUES DE L'ECRITURE BATAILLE/DERRIDA: le sens du sacré dans la pensée française du surréalisme à nos jours, par Jean-Michel Heimonet. 1987. (No. 229). *-9233-5.*

GOD, THE QUEST, THE HERO: THEMATIC STRUCTURES IN BECKETT'S FICTION, by Laura Barge. 1988. (No. 230). *-9235-1.*

THE NAME GAME. WRITING/FADING WRITER IN "DE DONDE SON LOS CANTANTES", by Oscar Montero. 1988. (No. 231). *-9236-X.*

GIL VICENTE AND THE DEVELOPMENT OF THE COMEDIA, by René Pedro Garay. 1988. (No. 232). *-9234-3.*

HACIA UNA POÉTICA DEL RELATO DIDÁCTICO: OCHO ESTUDIOS SOBRE "EL CONDE LUCANOR", por Aníbal A. Biglieri. 1989. (No. 233). *-9237-8.*

A POETICS OF ART CRITICISM: THE CASE OF BAUDELAIRE, by Timothy Raser. 1989. (No. 234). *-9238-6.*

UMA CONCORDÃNCIA DO ROMANCE "GRANDE SERTÃO: VEREDAS" DE JOÃO GUIMARÃES ROSA, by Myriam Ramsey and Paul Dixon. 1989. (No. 235). Microfiche, *-9239-4.*

CYCLOPEAN SONG: MELANCHOLY AND AESTHETICISM IN GÓNGORA S "FÁBULA DE POLIFEMO Y GALATEA", by Kathleen Hunt Dolan. 1990. (No. 236). *-9240-8.*

THE "SYNTHESIS" NOVEL IN LATIN AMERICA. A STUDY ON JOÃO GUIMARÃES ROSA'S "GRANDE SERTÃO: VEREDAS", by Eduardo de Faria Coutinho. 1991. (No. 237). *-9241-6.*

IMPERMANENT STRUCTURES. SEMIOTIC READINGS OF NELSON RODRIGUES' "VESTIDO DE NOIVA", "ÁLBUM DE FAMÍLIA", AND "ANJO NEGRO", by Fred M. Clark. 1991. (No. 238). *-9242-4.*

"EL ÁNGEL DEL HOGAR". GALDÓS AND THE IDEOLOGY OF DOMESTICITY IN SPAIN, by Bridget A. Aldaraca. 1991. (No. 239). *-9243-2.*

IN THE PRESENCE OF MYSTERY: MODERNIST FICTION AND THE OCCULT, by Howard M. Fraser. 1992. (No. 240). *-9244-0.*

THE NOBLE MERCHANT: PROBLEMS OF GENRE AND LINEAGE IN "HERVIS DE MES", by Catherine M. Jones. 1993. (No. 241). *-9245-9.*

JORGE LUIS BORGES AND HIS PREDECESSORS OR NOTES TOWARDS A MATERIALIST HISTORY OF LINGUISTIC IDEALISM, by Malcolm K. Read. 1993. (No. 242). *-9246-7.*

DISCOVERING THE COMIC IN "DON QUIXOTE", by Laura J. Gorfkle. 1993. (No. 243). *-9247-5.*

THE ARCHITECTURE OF IMAGERY IN ALBERTO MORAVIA'S FICTION, by Janice M. Kozma. 1993. (No. 244). *-9248-3.*

THE "LIBRO DE ALEXANDRE". MEDIEVAL EPIC AND SILVER LATIN, by Charles F. Fraker. 1993. (No. 245). *-9249-1.*

When ordering please cite the *ISBN Prefix* plus the last four digits for each title.

Send orders to: University of North Carolina Press
P.O. Box 2288
CB# 6215
Chapel Hill, NC 27515-2288
U.S.A.